WE BELIEVE IN GOD

A Report by The Doctrine Commission of the General Synod of the Church of England

1987

CHURCH HOUSE PUBLISHING
Church House, Great Smith Street, London SW1P 3NZ

ISBN 0 7151 3715 8

Published for the General Synod of the Church of England by Church House Publishing 1987

The Commission is indebted for much of the material in chapter 2 to *Licensed Insanities: Religions and Belief in God in the Contemporary World* by John Bowker, published and copyright 1987 by Darton, Longman and Todd Ltd, by whose permission the material is used.

Typesetting by Dorchester Typesetting Group Limited
Printed and bound in Great Britain by The Friary Press Limited,
Dorchester and London

Contents

In June 1986 the House of Bishops endorsed the recommendation of the Chairman of the Doctrine Commission that its reports should in future come before the House with a view to their publication under its authority.

This Report is the first to be published since that date. The House welcomes the Report and commends it to the Church.

On behalf of the House of Bishops
ROBERT CANTUAR:
Chairman

The Doctrine Commission
1981–1985

CHAIRMAN
The Right Revd John V. Taylor
Bishop of Winchester until 1985

MEMBERS
The Right Revd John A. Baker
Bishop of Salisbury; previously Canon of Westminster

The Revd Dr John Barton
Chaplain and Lecturer, St Cross College, Oxford

The Revd Dr Gareth Bennett
Fellow of New College and University Lecturer in Modern History, Oxford; Canon and Prebendary of Chichester

The Revd John Bowker
Dean of Trinity College, Cambridge; Honorary Canon of Canterbury; previously Professor of Religious Studies in the University of Lancaster

Dr Sarah Coakley
Lecturer in Religious Studies in the University of Lancaster

The Revd Dr John Halliburton
Priest-in-Charge of St Margaret's on Thames; previously Principal of Chichester Theological College; Canon and Prebendary of Chichester

The Revd Dr Anthony Harvey
Canon of Westminster; previously Chaplain of Queen's College and University Lecturer in Theology, Oxford

The Revd William Ind
Team Vicar of Basingstoke and Vice-Principal of the Aston Training Scheme; Honorary Canon of Winchester

The Revd Dr Barnabas Lindars, SSF
Rylands Professor of Biblical Criticism in the University of Manchester; Canon Theologian of Leicester

Dr Basil Mitchell, FBA
Nolloth Professor of the Philosophy of the Christian Religion and Fellow of Oriel College, Oxford

Dr Martin Rudwick
Professor of the History of Science, Princeton, USA; previously Fellow of Trinity College, Cambridge

The Revd Dr Stephen Smalley
Dean of Chester; previously Canon and Precentor of Coventry

The Revd Dr Anthony Thiselton
Principal of St John's College, Nottingham, and Special Lecturer in the University of Nottingham; previously Senior Lecturer in Biblical Studies in the University of Sheffield

The Revd William Vanstone
Canon Residentiary of Chester

The Revd John Goldingay, Registrar of St John's College, Nottingham, also joined the Commission but family illness compelled early withdrawal.

CONSULTANTS

The Right Revd Kenneth Cragg
formerly Assistant Bishop in Jerusalem

The Revd Dr Herbert McCabe, OP
of the Dominican Order, Blackfriars, Oxford

The Revd Dr George Newlands
Dean of Trinity Hall, Cambridge, and later Professor of Divinity in the University of Glasgow

SECRETARY

The Revd Michael Perham,
Chaplain to the Bishop of Winchester
succeeded in December 1984 by
The Revd John Meacham
Chaplain and Research Assistant to the Bishop of Salisbury

Chairman's Preface

The Report *Believing in the Church*, which appeared in 1981, marked the completion of a stage in which the Doctrine Commission had concentrated on questions of what it means for Christians, individually and corporately, to believe rather than on the content of belief. The lessons of that Report, and of its predecessor *Christian Believing* (1976), still need to be much more widely studied and absorbed in the Church of England. The Commission, however, considered that the time had come to start work on what Christians believe, and the present volume is the first fruits of this new programme.

My own position as Chairman in relation to this latest Report, *We Believe in God*, is an unusual one in that I have taken only a very minor part in the work. After the publication of *Believing in the Church* I resigned from the Commission, on preparing to move to my present post. Apart from one advisory contribution as a visiting consultant in 1983, and the actual editing of the Report for publication, I have not had the privilege of sharing in the project. All the creative work has been done by those whose names appear in the list on page v.

This, however, has the happy result of freeing me to thank and to congratulate all concerned for a very positive Report which many readers, I am sure, will find illuminating and enriching. It is not, and does not claim to be, a comprehensive survey either of all aspects of the Christian doctrine of God or of its complex history. Instead it focuses on particular aspects which the panel believed to be important both for churchpeople and for interested enquirers at the present time.

Chapter One begins from the point that belief in God continues to be a potent and widespread feature of human life today, which should challenge everyone to serious and open reflection. What does this belief entail? In Anglicanism the answer is traditionally sought through Scripture, Reason and the cumulative experience of Christians.

The Report is in some sense a bridge between the earlier publications already mentioned, which concentrated on the nature of believing, and the new programme of expounding the content of belief. Hence Chapters Two, Three and Four, though containing a good deal of the substance of the doctrine of God, also illuminate it by comparing it with the scientific enterprise, by examining the language in which it is expressed, and by surveying the way in which the Bible as a whole speaks to us about God.

Chapters Five and Six attempt to give a summary and synthesis of the major insights into the nature of God which are to be found in Scripture, while taking care also to bring out the distinctiveness of the various sources. The key to the Christian biblical understanding of God is Jesus Christ as believed in and proclaimed by the New Testament witnesses, who see him both as the fulfilment of past history and the determinant of the future.

So the argument passes on naturally to another characteristic element in Christian belief about God, the doctrine of the Trinity. In Chapter Seven, however, this is approached in an unusual way through the experience of Christian prayer; and the insights thus derived are traced further in the teaching of some of the Fathers. The question of gender in speaking of God is also brought out in this context.

Chapter Eight then earths what has been said so far in experiences of life and worship. It is a mark of the Christian God that he can be known only from within a response of loving obedience to his call. Various forms of such obedience – in daily life, prayer, worship, personal relationships – are examined, culminating in reflection on the Eucharist and its relation to our service of God's world.

The final chapter seeks to face the ultimate question: can we believe in God as controller of that world and, as such, worthy of our trust? After examining various biblical models, the issue of the suffering of God is confronted, and belief in an impassible God discarded. The fulfilment of God's purpose for good in an eternal order is achieved only along the way of Cross and Resurrection which God himself has walked.

It is important to emphasise that the Report is unanimous, and that no part of the book carries the name of an individual author. *Believing in the Church* also had the unanimous support of the whole Commission, but final decisions as to the wording of each essay, after it had been carefully reviewed by all the members collectively, rested with the individual author. The entire text, however, of *We Believe in God* has been agreed by the whole panel. This does not mean that individual members would not, left to themselves, have worded this or that differently, but that all are prepared to stand behind every sentence of the text as printed.

This is a very considerable achievement on the part of all concerned, but especially of the Chairman who initiated the project and guided it to completion, John Taylor, till 1985 Bishop of Winchester. To him all of us would wish to pay the most heartfelt tribute of gratitude and admiration. In theological thinking inexhaustibly creative, in love and devotion an inspiring friend and colleague, his leadership has been of decisive significance for the Commission's work. *Believing in the Church* has been widely recognised as a major contribution to the Church of England's task of intellectual discipleship. We hope that *We Believe in God* will also be recognised as a worthy memorial of his dedicated service as head of the Commission.

With *Believing in the Church* the Doctrine Commission regained recognition as an advisory body to which the House of Bishops of the General Synod could refer questions with clearly theological implications. Now this latest Report, having been submitted to the House of Bishops for their approval, has been officially commended by them to the Church for study. It is the hope of all those who work with the Commission in any capacity that in the years ahead it may continue and develop this kind of service to the Church at large.

The writings of the Doctrine Commission cannot be 'popular' in every sense of that overworked word. We hope however that *We Believe in God* will be accessible to a large number of interested readers. We hope also that, where appropriate, it will be possible for the Commission's ideas to be communicated to a still wider readership through simplified versions, study guides and so forth, prepared by qualified people.

Finally, on behalf of the Commission, may I express our warmest thanks to those who have helped in various invaluable ways in the creation of this Report, but who are not in any sense to be burdened with responsibility for its defects. First, to our Consultants, who made an important ecumenical as well as scholarly contribution; then to our two Secretaries, the Reverend Michael Perham, who served for most of the work, and his successor, the Reverend John Meacham; to Miss Keri Lewis of the General Synod Office, for her most generous assistance at all times; and to Mrs Pauline Wood, for secretarial support at our residential meetings.

+JOHN SARUM

1

Towards a Doctrine of God

'I believe in God'. Throughout this country there are individuals and communities who gather together day by day, or week by week, to praise and worship God, to pray to him and learn about him, and to be renewed in human goodness. Many are Christians; many who affirm belief in God are adherents of other faiths. Alongside these again are countless others who are only distantly or precariously attached to the forms and institutions of existing religions but who acknowledge a sense of the reality of God. Outward observances may have changed, church attendance may have declined. But religious belief and practice are still among the facts which need to be accounted for in the world of today. Nowhere has God left himself without a witness. Everywhere there are people who believe in him.

But how does one go on from there? What is this God like in whom so many people believe? What can I say about him which will give sharper definition to my belief without leading me into the error of supposing that I can reduce him to what can be caught in the net of human language? Am I still justified in believing in him despite all those apparent obstacles to belief which the modern world insistently thrusts upon my attention? In the face of the atrocities as well as the human achievements of this century, can I go on thinking of him as all-powerful, all-knowing, perfectly good? On what grounds do I prefer the Christian account of God to those of other faiths? And is that Christian account with, for example, the one-sided masculinity of its picture of God still one I can properly accept? In short, what is my doctrine of God?

1

These are some of the questions to which this book will be addressed. But it is important to ask at the outset what kind of answer it is reasonable to expect. The previous report of the Doctrine Commission, *Believing in the Church*, argued that it is a mistake to think of anyone's religious belief as if it were a piece of private property. Belief is a shared possession. It cannot be acquired simply from private meditation and reflection; it cannot be parcelled up in a book and handed to people to take as much or as little of it as they will. It starts from an inheritance which is the common property of countless men and women to whom it has been handed down through many generations. It is the fruit of the faithful response and search of communities as much as of the internal illumination and wrestling of individuals. It is again and again found to be not just the conclusion of an argument, but also the basis of a whole set of values, a whole way of looking at things. It may involve each person in a lone quest of conscience, a sustained venture of prayer, a private journey not only of seeking but of being sought and found. But it also enlists the believer in a common enterprise, in the shared receiving of a gift, in a corporate experience of worship and a joint endeavour of service in a community. Again and again it will be more appropriate to say (as the Church has today learned afresh to do), not 'I believe' but 'We believe'.

It follows that it will not be sufficient, when presenting a doctrine of God, merely to offer a set of beliefs which it would be reasonable for someone to adopt in the light of the Christian revelation and of the present state of human knowledge. The starting-point is not the possibility of believing in God but the fact of it. Many millions of people believe in a God of some kind; particular beliefs about God are held by Christians; and specific forms of these beliefs may be held by members of the Church of England. But it is no simple matter to identify these, or to set them out in a coherent statement. Even an exhaustive enquiry of every church member, to find out what they believed, would still not be able to answer the question 'what the Church believes'. Nor can one read off the answer from the Scriptures and the official formularies of the Church. It is true that there are statements about God which are frequently repeated and are generally accepted by church members: for example, that he is creator of heaven and earth, that he is one to whom all hearts are open, all desires known, that he is the Father of our Lord Jesus Christ. But the mere recital of these phrases will not answer all the questions nor yield a 'doctrine of God'. For that it is necessary to know how they are interpreted by believers today, in what order of priority they stand, and how far the language in which they are expressed is used in a way compatible with modern understanding. Only then will they supply material for answering the question, 'What is the Christian doctrine of God?'

THE USE OF SCRIPTURE

How, then, does one begin to identify that doctrine? Why not start with that which seems to give the most specific and authoritative information about God – Holy Scripture itself? Part of what it means to be a Christian is the acceptance of the Bible as a unique revelation of the nature and activity of God. It should be possible, therefore, at least in theory, to read off a doctrine of God from its pages.

This has, of course, often been attempted. But such attempts do not result in a doctrine of God which then becomes accepted, without further discussion, by the community of believers. The Bible is not the kind of book which can easily be made to yield a single and consistent doctrine. It consists of a large number of attempts to speak about God and to 'read' the world and human existence in the light of a belief in God, arising from various situations in the history and experience, first of the people of Israel, and then of the Christian Church. Certain fundamental beliefs, such as that God is one, and that he is the creator of all that is, run right through it. But the more carefully one studies the Bible, the more one becomes aware of ideas of God and responses to him which seem actually to conflict with one another. Thus, God is a righteous judge, who does not protect his creatures from the consequences of their sins, but God is also a loving Father, who will not abandon his people even when they rebel against him. God is awesome and holy, infinitely removed from the sphere of his sinful creatures, yet God is also known with great directness and intimacy by those who approach him with penitence and love. God is a God of peace and non-violence: but acts of great severity, even of brutality, are attributed to him.

In the face of these apparent contradictions, the sceptic may well doubt whether Scripture can be relied on to give authoritative guidance at all. But the believer who finds in the Bible a convincing experience of God and an authentic inspiration is not disposed to withdraw confidence from it so easily. The Bible's own positive qualities are so strong that it is reasonable to look for explanations of its apparent inconsistencies. It has often been argued, for example, that the Bible is a record of a developing faith, so that the more 'primitive' may be discarded in favour of the more 'advanced'; or that apparent contradictions are no more than exaggerations of emphasis, ensuring that essential aspects of the nature of God are not overlooked, the resolution of these inevitable tensions being part of the ultimate mystery of God himself. But whatever response is adopted, the consequence is likely to be different nuances of understanding and different stances on matters of faith and conduct among church members.

Sometimes these differences can be contained within one community of believers. The Church has, for example, very largely been able to embrace those who think that a Christian may legitimately take up arms and those who do not. Sometimes, however, differences lead to the forma-tion of sects and denominations, which become separated in a way that causes grief and offence to Christians and evokes derision from outsiders. It simply is not possible to go 'back to the Scriptures' to re-establish a faith that is 'true' in every particular – attempts to do so usually result in the formation of yet another sect, proclaiming the correctness of its interpretation against all comers. Doctrine can be successfully formulated only from within a community which already shares certain options out of the range of possible interpretations, and has entrenched this 'tradition' in its style of worship, thought and conduct. On many matters there is general agreement among all the main Christian Churches; in these cases appeal can be made to the historic tradition of the Church. But on others – and by no means always significant ones – different convictions are held both between and within denominations. It is in this sense that one may talk not just of the Christian but of, for example, the Anglican – or even the Church of England – 'doctrine of God'.

There is no reason to think that it must be some defect in Christian revelation which results in such divergences. Any 'scripture' is by definition something written at a particular period in a particular language and cultural setting. Even at the level of translation, it may be impossible to replace a word in one language with another from a different language-system without involving some change of meaning. Distance in historical time or in cultural context makes this problem more acute. Hence a message or event in the course of time is bound to become subject to divergent interpretations even if this was not so at the beginning. All religions with sacred writings tend to have the same problem. It is instructive, for instance, to consider the situation in Islam. There scripture is in principle considerably more unified and homogeneous than the Bible, and is expected to regulate belief and conduct with an undisputed inerrancy. Yet several sects have issued from it, each claiming to have the 'true' interpretation, and often bitterly opposed to the others, sometimes even to the point of armed conflict.

If Christianity, along with other great religions, believes that God has revealed himself through the medium of human speech and recorded words, then it cannot look for fixed, normative and universally agreed doctrine. Christians may continue to honour the fundamental role of Scripture in their access to knowledge of God. But they need also to recognise (and this is an important part of the Anglican tradition) the part played by human judgement and experience in the work of formulating the beliefs derived from it. Indeed, one of the fruits of modern critical study of the Bible has been to reveal the extent to which these factors were already present in the formation of Scripture itself.

THE ROLE OF REASON

What resources do Christians bring to this constant engagement with revealed truth? First, and most obviously, their powers of reason. In Western culture all are to some extent children of Plato and Aristotle. It is taken for granted that all authentic knowledge of anything in the universe should be capable of being expressed in some logically coherent system. Believers, therefore, naturally assume that the same will be true of knowledge of God. God will not violate human categories of thought. This is a significant assumption to make about one who, by definition, transcends them. Not all the world's religions make this assumption. Mystics, even in the Christian tradition, seem sometimes to call it into question when they resort to paradox in an attempt to communicate their experience – though it should be remembered that paradox is not the same as the non-sense of self-contradiction. Nevertheless, whatever other options are theoretically possible, this is the assumption on which Christian theology is traditionally based; and that is why the logically trained mind continues to have an important part to play in constructing the Christian doctrine of God.

There is a long history of Christian debate over the precise function of human reason in this process. Some have thought of it as a kind of arbiter, with the task only of ensuring that any formulation of revealed truth should be compatible with the demands of reason; others have given reason a more creative role, believing that by observation of the universe it can actually supplement the knowledge of God that is available from revelation. But whichever side is taken, there can be no doubt about the importance of reason itself. Indeed, from the beginning, questions about the doctrine of God have engaged the most brilliant minds in the Church.

Yet it is here that belief in God may seem most vulnerable today. Reason does not demand merely that a doctrine of God should be logically coherent in itself. It demands also that the truths it asserts should be compatible with other truths, derived from observation. This is the point at which believers can find themselves most strongly challenged by developments (or seeming developments) in many fields of human knowledge. Thus, there was a time a few years ago when philosophy appeared to have called in question the very possibility of making meaningful statements about anything which could not be empirically verified. The sociology of knowledge seems often to imply that all knowledge of anything is decisively conditioned by upbringing, culture and environment. There is a dramatically enlarging body of valid scientific knowledge, with a correspondingly increased potential for ever more precise prediction, and an explosive expansion in technologies of every kind, which both threaten to dominate human life and at the same time seem almost to promise a solution to all human problems. From all this has sprung a radical questioning of such ideas as providence, moral freedom and responsibility, or the possibility of change under the influence of God. To many, belief in God seems bound to retreat before these attacks. The attempts made by believers to consolidate their position, or to pick off their assailants one by one, seem to them little more than a postponement of the inevitable collapse.

But believers cannot see it like this. Their belief in God enables them to make sense of far more of their experience than science or philosophy ever could. Indeed they find they have allies within those disciplines themselves. The fact that scientists or philosophers may be Christian does not mean that they are either myopic or naive. Knowing their subjects from the inside, they see better than most, not only their own limitations, but also the significant analogies which exist between their own field of enquiry and that of religious thought and practice. Of course, the believer must be careful not to make too much of this. The fact that a scientist may be a Christian does not in itself tilt the balance of the argument between science and Christianity. The scientist may simply have failed (or not been willing) to use the same powers of analysis on religion as he or she would bring to observation of the natural world. Nevertheless, the believing scientist may provide valuable help by showing that belief and science need not be at war at all, if the proper scope and methods of each are understood. Believer and scientist each stand before immense mysteries. As each discerns better the magnitude of their field of enquiry, they become less of a threat to each other, and may even discover areas of fruitful collaboration. We shall argue that in the last resort a comparable act of faith is demanded of each. That both still find it possible to make this act of faith suggests that it should be no more difficult now than it was before for reason to accept the existence of the realities in which each believes – the reality of God, and the reality of a universe accessible to human understanding.

THE APPEAL TO EXPERIENCE

But reason is not the only resource which the community of believers brings to bear on its inheritance of revealed truth. Those who believe in God seldom rely on rational thought alone. They testify to a variety of 'religious experiences', from a general sense of the holy or numinous on the one hand to a sensation of being directly addressed by a transcendent being on the other. Such experiences are notoriously hard to evaluate. To some they seem an irrefutable authentication of belief in God; to others they appear dangerously subjective, to be regarded at most as provisional confirmation of belief held on other grounds. Indeed, as with reason, so with religious experience: some regard it as making a significant contribution to our knowledge of God, others as offering only certain marginal considerations of which belief in God must take some account. Moreover, not only is such experience open to the charge of being subjective, it also appears to be unequal, if not haphazard, in its distribution. Many profound believers claim to be ignorant of it; many powerful experiences fail to result in a solid faith. Nevertheless, the fact remains that in twentieth-century England many thousands of people continue to pray and to worship in the conviction that in doing so they have personal experience of God, while many others believe themselves to be addressed, guided or protected by some supernatural power. Such experience is often ambiguous, and cannot stand on its own as an argument for the existence of God. But it is right to take account of it as one of the factors which cause people to return to the sources of their religious tradition, and which give them confidence in the truth of what they have received; and later chapters will return to it in more detail.

THE SEARCH FOR MEANING

Believing in the Church was an attempt to study the interaction of these three factors – revelation, reason and experience – in the life of the Church, and the influence of this perpetual conversation on the formulation of doctrine. To use this approach in trying to determine what is believed – or ought to be believed – about God, is a difficult and complex task, and one that can yield only a provisional result, since the conversation is still going on and will continue to do so for as long as the Church exists. If it were to die down, and positions once established came to be regarded as no longer open to question, the task of a Doctrine Commission would be very much easier, and many people would doubtless feel more secure in their faith. But such definition and stability could be purchased only at the cost of severely reduced vitality in the Church. The Church's life is nourished by the interplay between that which it has received from the past and that which it experiences and reflects on in the present. This interplay is like a conversation between, on the one hand, the relatively fixed historic revelation received and passed down by the Church, and, on the other, all the constantly changing observations and thoughts which need to be related to that revelation, together with the immense variety of religious experience.

It is important not to oversimplify. Revelation may be less of a fixed point than it appears; and one of the reasons why critical scholarship has so often seemed threatening to faith is that it seems to open up so many possible interpretations of the Church's foundation documents. Equally, both reason and religious experience display continuities with the past as well as innovations. Yet a degree of polarisation certainly exists and can be observed in most churches today. In the face of contemporary challenges, some believers instinctively seek to consolidate their base of revealed truths and to stay close to traditional formulations. Others take the contest further afield than has ever been ventured before, and allow contemporary thought-forms and experiences to impose such drastically new interpretations on traditional formulations that their surprised fellow-Christians may feel justified in asking whether they still believe in God at all. This kind of tension is, in our view, a sign of vitality in the Church. It is a sign that belief in God, far from being gradually excluded by the modern world, is still robust enough both to challenge and to respond to the thinking of that world, and thus to testify to the reality of the God whom Christians proclaim.

But not only Christians. If the construction of a doctrine of God were merely a process of inference from the data of Christian Scripture and tradition, it would be an exclusive, almost domestic, matter, to be discussed only by those who already have a Christian commitment. But if, as has been argued, both reason and experience have an essential part to play, the field becomes much wider. It is part of the history of the Church of England that, as a national Church, it has maintained some kind of contact (sometimes uneasy, sometimes fruitful) with a large number of people who, though they might well not call themselves Christians, nevertheless continue to 'read' the universe in a way that postulates the existence of God. They may find that the arguments for the Christian religion, or for any religion, fail to persuade them. They may have had no experience which they would recognise as 'religious'. But they persist in searching for some meaning in human life and history, in the natural world and in personal relationships, which cannot be provided by any purely human or scientific analysis.

This search for meaning takes many different forms, and no single phenomenon in our human environment can be relied on to satisfy it. Some find that beauty, such as that of a sunrise, or the song of a skylark or a butterfly's wing discloses to them the meaning of things. Some go further, and describe the experience as a kind of personal communication which took them by surprise: they did not initiate it, it was as if they were being addressed by someone or something outside themselves. Yet at other times similar phenomena can have the opposite effect. Nature is seen as 'red in tooth and claw' – and the more vividly since the arrival of new photographic techniques. With their help brilliant TV programmes bring home to us aspects of nature we usually prefer to ignore: the way one species feeds on another, or the insignificance of the individual creature in the struggle for survival – the kind of thing which (as Charles Gore said of a visit to the zoo) should 'make one an atheist in twenty minutes'. But still the search for meaning goes on, and will not easily be either repelled or satisfied.

It is true that in the West today there is an unprecedented number of people who seem to be willing, consciously or unconsciously, to embrace a materialist view of the world. They gratefully enjoy the advantages offered by technology, and the relative security provided by insurance schemes. They accept the palliatives, tranquillisers and diversions offered by modern society to help them in times of adversity, and regard any search for meaning beyond this as irrelevant and illusory. For many, especially perhaps if for the first time they are experiencing comparative prosperity and freedom from imposed authority, this appears to be a satisfying option; and those who try to awaken in them the life of the spirit find themselves daunted and mystified by the apparent absence of any sense of need or questioning. Personal calamities can of course profoundly affect this sense of satisfaction, and reveal an inner vulnerability and a desperate need for less materialist values. But it would be wrong to deny that a marked indifference to humanity's historic search for meaning has become characteristic of industrially developed societies in many parts of the world.

Yet there remain at least as many people who will not or cannot rid themselves of the thirst for meaning. Experiencing an overwhelming sense of dislocation in the world in which they live, they seek to cope with this in various ways. Some look back to the recent, or even distant, past, and hold on to the meaning and values they remember – or imagine – as obtaining then. Others become passionately concerned with particular issues and causes that give them a reason for living which is greater than themselves. Others adopt alternative life-styles, private or communal, deliberately isolated from the utilitarian and materialist principles which seem to them to govern social and public affairs. Others again may become persuaded that their thirst for meaning can never be satisfied, and be oppressed by that desolating sense of futility to which so much modern art bears eloquent witness.

This refusal to be reconciled to meaninglessness is both widespread and pervasive. At the popular level, sociological surveys of 'implicit' or 'residual' religion reveal the tenacity with which traditional ways of 'reading' the world are held. Among intellectuals, literature and drama continue to express the condition beautifully expressed in Salman Rushdie's novel *Midnight's Children*, where it is said of a Muslim doctor that 'he was knocked forever into that middle place, unable to worship a God in whose existence he could not wholly disbelieve'. It is tempting to use such a prevalent phenomenon as an argument, even if a negative one, for the reality of the God whose 'death' is mourned so inconsolably. If there were indeed no God, then this ought to be a passing phase consequent upon the breakdown of a dominant religious culture, a temporary nostalgia destined to be grown out of. Yet in fact, even in Marxist and 'post-Christian' cultures, it seems to be intensifying rather than declining. At the very least, this thirst for meaning is a factor which must be taken account of in any serious presentation of a doctrine of God. The evidence points to there being still many people whose sense of need is exactly that of St Augustine: 'our heart is restless till it rests in thee'.

THE IMPACT OF OTHER FAITHS

In England today, more often than ever before, Christians find that they have neighbours who pray and worship in ways and in language not unlike their own, but who profess a different religion and whose doctrine of God is very different. Again, it is important not to claim too much for the existence of these adherents of other faiths as evidence in the battle against unbelief. Adding to the number of those who profess belief does not alter the balance of the argument about God. It is logically possible that all are equally deluded in thinking that alleged experience or inherited religious teachings and practices point to the existence of a Reality outside ourselves. But it is certainly right to think of them as allies, in the sense that they are engaged on the same enterprise. They too are attempting to 'read' the universe, and to evaluate their own experience, in the light of an inherited revelation. We believe that the Christian revelation is true in many respects in which theirs is false. But there is also much in Christian and other traditions which overlaps – enough to suggest that all are in touch in some degree with a single reality which, in these different idioms, is acknowledged and worshipped as God. They can become part of the resources of reason and experience which help to make explicit the doctrine of God implied in our own Scripture and tradition; and this should lead us to show openness and reverence towards the beliefs and practices of others. We may conclude (as is the case in much missionary thinking today) that the appropriate Christian stance towards them is to listen, and to engage in dialogue on equal terms. Such an attitude need not imply indifference to the question of the truth and the uniqueness of the Christian revelation, but it can greatly widen our view of the resources available to interpret and explore that revelation, and of the human potential which that revelation may be able to release.

CONTEMPORARY CHALLENGES AND CONSTRAINTS

Many factors in the world today are pressing Christians to speak in new ways about God. Every theology involves a decision about priorities. The historic creeds sum up the mind of the Church on what it seemed most important to say about God at the time; and these priorities, focused in creation, salvation and judgement, remained unquestioned until the end of the Middle Ages, and have continued to provide a fixed point of reference for Christian belief to the present day. The Reformation introduced new concerns: the necessity of personal repentance, the supremacy of grace, and justification by faith alone. These became matters of supreme importance, and were duly incorporated in confessional formulations of belief which were used in addition to the creeds. In modern times yet other priorities have emerged. The threat of a totalitarian regime in Germany was answered by a new emphasis on the autonomous authority of the Christian revelation, given classic expression in the Barmen Declaration of 1934; and the flagrant economic and social injustices of the modern world have now evoked a doctrine of God's 'preferential option for the poor'.

Meanwhile yet other historical developments are calling into question ways of speaking about God which have been taken for granted for centuries. Was it a man-dominated culture which led to neglect of those feminine aspects of God which are alluded to in the Bible itself? Are

14

traditional Christian approaches to suffering and evil adequate in the face of the horrors of the holocaust and the threat of nuclear annihilation?

None of this means, of course, that the Church is free to formulate its doctrine of God in any way that meets the exigent demands of the modern world. Christians are concerned ultimately not with a doctrine of God but with God himself, who has made himself known in the unique revelation of his Son, and continues to be present in a great variety of ways to those who pray and worship and who seek to serve and understand him. We are concerned, that is to say, with an ultimate Reality which we believe to exist, and to which we claim to have privileged access through the Scriptures and tradition preserved for us by the Church. But in seeking to go beyond the mere statement that 'We believe in God', and to be more precise about what kind of a God he is, we join a conversation which has been in progress since the beginning of the Christian religion, and which in various forms must be conducted within any 'revealed religion' if that religion is to remain alive.

As was argued in *Believing in the Church*, it cannot be the task of a Doctrine Commission to capture this process in a still shot, and to say 'This you may (or must) believe'. The Commission's work is part of the process itself, and its claim on the attention of church members is not that it has been given special authority to define doctrine, but rather that it has been asked to report and comment on the present state of our Church's wrestling with the tradition we have received, and to do so in the light of recent developments in theology and of the insights and challenges offered by the world today. The Commission can try to indicate legitimate areas of debate and uncertainty; but it can also use such authority as it possesses to support all those whose life, worship and testimony affirm that the fundamental doctrines which the Church has received from the past can be confidently believed and proclaimed today. It is for these reasons that a substantial part of this Report has deliberately been devoted to matters which might seem to have more to do with the contribution of religious experience than of speculative thought.

This is not to say that religious phenomena should always be judged positively. Religious zeal can become fanaticism, and result, as so often today, in strife and bloodshed. Religious conviction can degenerate into bigotry, and breed intolerance and bitterness. A passion for religious truth can produce a jealous sectarianism which is yet another cause of division in today's tragically divided world. But the fact that the debate about God can degenerate into such tragic consequences does not mean that it must do so. Indeed, part of the purpose of this book is to help to resolve within the Church of England the kind of antagonisms which arise in any Church from powerful religious experiences, as well as to offer secure grounds for the faith of those who claim to have had little or no such experience at all. Nevertheless, experience is an important element in the constant dialogue which the Church maintains with the data it has inherited from Scripture and tradition. The continuance and vitality of this dialogue make it reasonable to say that those who engage in it must be arguing about something and not nothing. In the same way, the persistence of worship, prayer and lives of service and dedication in so many communities of faith, despite the powerful pressures and ideologies ranged against them, makes the debate about God still the most important question confronting humankind today.

2

God and Our Ways of Knowing

CHALLENGES TO BELIEVING IN GOD

The opening chapter drew attention to the fact – since it is a fact – that individuals and communities, in all parts of the world and in great numbers, gather together for the worship of God, and for the renewing of their lives according to his will. This is something that is happening now, day by day, week by week, in all parts of the world, despite many claims that belief in God is a fading shadow at the end of the ages of faith. Such claims are manifestly false.

What certainly is true is that the activity of believing in God goes on in the context of a world which is often, and in different ways, hostile to it. An extreme example of one way is the explicit attack of Marxist regimes on the practice of religion outside the boundaries of what they define as 'freedom of religion'. A very different form of attack is the way in which believing in God is still called in question, as it always has been, by the facts of pain, evil and suffering. 'How are atheists produced?', asked Bernard Shaw. 'In probably nine cases out of ten, what happens is something like this. A beloved wife or husband or child or sweetheart is gnawed to death by cancer, stultified by epilepsy, struck dumb and helpless by apoplexy, or strangled by croup or diphtheria; and the looker-on, after praying vainly to God to refrain from such horrible and wanton cruelty, indignantly repudiates faith in the divine monster, and becomes not merely indifferent and sceptical, but fiercely and actively hostile to religion.'

That hostility may then be very powerfully reinforced by the accumulating history of wicked and evil deeds which have been done specifically in the name of God, and often with an appeal for his blessing on them. 'There is no social evil, no form of injustice, whether of the feudal or the capitalist order, which has not been sanctified in some way or another by religious sentiment and thereby rendered more impervious to change.' Those words were written, not by a paid-up member of an anti-God union, but by a Christian philosopher much concerned with the social implications of Christianity, Reinhold Niebuhr.

As if all that were not enough to call in question the sanity of believing in God, what of all the many doubts raised by the explorations and achievements of human intelligence? How can traditional beliefs survive when they are called in question in so many different ways? How, for example, is it possible to believe that God can intervene or answer prayer in a universe such as contemporary physics and cosmology imagine it to be? Where, in the process of evolution, does the animal become human in such a way that there can be attributed to it a soul? What is the soul, anyway? What now can we possibly imagine will survive the death and decay of this particular body? Does a belief in incarnation imply that God is a visitor, not from outer space, but from outside the time-space continuum of this particular universe altogether? If so, how can such a belief be intelligible?

It would be easy to add to such a list of questions. What we sometimes overlook is that none of them is new. They are asked with new content and therefore with a different cutting edge. But the fact remains that it was always hard to see how God could be a participant in the events culminating in the fifth century in the sack of Rome, the disaster which motivated Augustine to write *The City of God*; or again, what part he could play in the highly mechanistic universe of Newtonian physics. Then there are other questions: how do human beings, who change so much from birth to death, nevertheless retain their individual identity through time? How are body, brain and mind related? What is the nature of the self and the soul? All these are issues with which thinking people have been concerned for thousands of years in both the Eastern and the Western worlds. And the conclusions to which they have come have, of course, been very diverse.

Does this then mean that we are in such a muddle about everything that we cannot know much about anything? No, but it does mean that our knowledge is a great deal more limited and incomplete than we usually suppose as space shuttles take off and land, as kidneys are transplanted, or our teeth are attended to with much less pain than our great-grandparents had to endure. It also means that many of the arguments and issues are still open, not only about ourselves but also about God. Despite some strong claims to the contrary, it is not true that we now know for certain that God has no reality independent of ourselves, and that to talk of 'God' is consequently no more than a way of encouraging ourselves to live more responsibly, more hopefully, more lovingly in the world.

Of course, to some people, particularly within various movements in thought and philosophy, the issues have seemed settled. Nietzsche, for example, declared the death of God as a recent event in 1887. More recently, logical positivists claimed that any statement purporting to refer to a matter of fact was meaningless, unless it could meet the demands of what they termed the verifiability criterion (roughly, that it must be tied directly or indirectly to some observation). Clearly, theology does not produce God as an object to be observed; therefore, theology was claimed to be meaningless. For A. J. Ayer, a leading advocate of logical positivism, as in a different way for Nietzsche, the debate about the reality of God was over. The issue was closed.

The challenge of logical positivism to theology, and to the claim that it does make sense to speak of the God whom we trust and to whom we pray, was immensely powerful earlier this century. Those who lived through the period with some knowledge of what was going on will certainly remember the searching questions it raised for their own faith. But time and philosophy move on. In a remarkable moment during a recent TV series ('Men of Ideas') on some creators of contemporary philosophy, Bryan Magee asked A. J. Ayer: 'It [logical positivism] must have had real defects. What do you now, in retrospect, think the main ones were?' Ayer replied: 'Well, I suppose the most important of the defects was that nearly all of it was false.'

What do we conclude from that? Certainly not that, provided we wait long enough, all these irritants will subside and disappear, and that present ways of thinking about God, or of trying to understand the demands he makes on our life and commitment, can go happily on, much as they did before. Many ways of imagining or describing or thinking about what we hold to be true, either of God or of the universe, will sooner or later turn out to be incomplete and in some respects wrong. Earth's proud empires pass away; so do its cosmologies, philosophies, anthropologies, psychologies, theologies, technologies and all the rest. But in all or most of these there can be irreversible gains, genuine and enduring achievements. Not everything is swept away. Logical positivism, in its classical form, may have been 'mostly false', but no philosopher can any longer write philosophy as he might have attempted to do before – without, that is, an enhanced sensitivity to the constraints and possibilities of language. There are irreversible gains in technology. One hundred and fifty years ago we were travelling by stage-coach, now by train, bus, bike or car; but we do not have to reinvent the wheel each time. This is not to imply that all such gains are to be equated uncritically with 'progress' in the sense of human betterment. It is simply to observe that, despite the incompleteness of human knowledge, we say and do many things with a confidence accumulated through time. And that is true also of what we say and do in relation to God.

Although our knowledge, therefore, is necessarily incomplete and in general open to correction, a great many judgements and actions are reasonably and reliably based.

That is true, not just of philosophy or physics or technology, but also of theology – of what we say as a consequence of believing in God. We are entitled – and often on reflection required – to make some judgements, and to do so with confidence: that God first loved us before we loved him; that nothing can separate us from the love of God in Christ Jesus our Lord.

Such judgements do not arrive from nowhere: they arrive in the context of history and community; they arrive also, in the religious case, in the form of revelation, in words and actions and events which are revelatory of God, and not a matter merely of human invention. Consequently, those who live later in time do not have to rediscover or reinvent these things for themselves, any more than we have to rediscover the wheel.

No one can live without trusting (however critically) the communities that surround and precede them; and that remains true, no matter how often that trust is betrayed. The indispensable importance of believing, and of doing so not in detachment but in community, was explored in the report *Believing in the Church*. What is being explored in this chapter is a strange and curious paradox. Irreversible gains and highly reliable judgements are made and recognised, as much in theology or Christian living as in philosophy, technology, history, and so on. Yet they are made by those who are, to say the least, fallible, and who are limited by their time and circumstances. How can it make sense to claim that we do make reliable and trustworthy judgements, when so much of what we say or believe may be (as Ayer said of logical positivism) nearly all false?

THE RELIABILITY OF KNOWLEDGE

It may help to pursue a little further the example of science, not least because so many people assume that it is in the sciences that knowledge is reasonably complete and certain. Yet in fact science is a prime example of a field in which genuine, irreversible gains in human understanding are combined with accounts of reality which are unquestionably incomplete, provisional, approximate and open to correction. What is more, this is not a situation which can be overcome simply by correcting our ignorance. We must now accept that in the very nature of things it will always be like that.

This is a very new situation. Only about a hundred years ago it seemed that a complete description of the universe and its workings could be given in terms of Newtonian laws and principles. The universe was regarded as a vast machine of such regularity that, if the state and position of all its components at any given moment could be known, its whole future could be predicted. We now realise that this is impossible not just in practice, but in principle. At the quantum level (describing and explaining physical phenomena below the dimensions of atoms) it is impossible, from however complete a description of the universe, fully to predict the behaviour of all its parts. We 'disturb the universe' when we observe it at this level. In making a precise measurement of momentum it becomes impossible to make the related observation of position to the same degree of precision, and vice versa. A consequence of what is in fact known as 'the uncertainty principle' (and the name itself makes the point) is that we live in a universe such that our view of it is affected by the procedures through which we attempt to observe or measure it. Knowledge at this level can never be complete.

Some philosophers of science and sociologists of knowledge have pressed the point even further. They have argued that whatever the universe may ultimately be like in itself, we can know it only through our theories, language, models and equations. None of these is able to reproduce the whole of what there really is, out there, waiting, as it were, to be described. We can only construct through our pictures or theories (whether of common-sense or of science) how it seems to us. Half a century ago the physicist and cosmologist Arthur Eddington began his Gifford lectures on *The Nature of the Physical World* by asking: Is this table a comparatively permanent, coloured and substantial object, or is it a swarm of atoms which is nearly all empty space? It is, of course, both – and more than both – depending on the human context in which we encounter what we call a table, and our purposes in using or examining it. If we are sitting at it to write a letter or eat a meal, or appreciating the style of Chippendale furniture, our descriptions of the table will be quite different – but no less valid – than those we would construct in a laboratory while studying the micro-structure of mahogany or the behaviour of carbon isotopes. At the same time, the micro-structural description, arrived at by the testing of a model (see p.27 below), must explain the commonsense appearance and properties of the table.

There may, therefore, be an indefinite number of accounts of a given reality, all of which are equally 'true' on their own terms. But it does not follow that any account of that reality will be as true as any other. There is some limit set over our language and our ways of imagining or thinking about the universe – a limit which is not of our own construction, but which arises from persistence and regularity in the behaviours or events which we observe (and that remains true, even when we affect the events or behaviours by our own involvement in them). That is why the worlds we live in are so reliable: you can reliably expect to fall to the ground if you step off the roof of a house; you can reliably expect to produce carbolic acid if you fuse sodium benzenesulfonate with sodium hydroxide; you can reliably expect the sun to rise tomorrow (note the conventional and strictly corrigible language), although logically you cannot be certain of it.

It follows that reliability, to be worth having, does not have to reach a degree of absolute certainty. Very different degrees and kinds of reliability are attained (and are found to be reliable) in an immense variety of different enterprises. They emerge in such things as science, history, commonsense, sociology, the administration of justice, marriage, economics, orienteering, doing the pools; whereas in some enterprises (e.g. the popular, and perhaps all, forms of astrology) there is no reliability at all. Where the sciences are concerned, the constant probing and testing of reliability, generation by generation, makes them what the American psychologist, Donald Campbell, has called 'well-winnowed traditions'. To winnow is to sift the grain from the chaff; and it is by this process of sifting and testing that the sciences become well-winnowed traditions of great reliability, while still remaining provisional, corrigible and incomplete. They can never be known to give a final account of 'how the universe really is'. That may always lie beyond us. But they can give accounts which are highly reliable for particular purposes, and they can eliminate some other accounts as failing in coherence or correspondence or reference or reliability or usefulness or validity – or whatever else may be involved in truth.

That scientific knowledge is so profoundly corrigible runs counter to the popular assumption that it is the only valid way of knowing anything. The corrigibility of science can lead (and in fact has led) to massive corrections of its own past or present: the sequence from Newton's absolutes of space and time to Einstein and relativity, to Bohr and quantum mechanics, is an instructive example of this process. It also illustrates the vital point that Newton did not suddenly become 'wrong' overnight. The older theory remains valid enough (in the kind of time and space in which human beings live) for it to be highly reliable for many practical purposes. The operational success of satellites and space probes is a witness to the enduring validity of Newton's laws, even though in other ways his conception of the physical universe has long been superseded by the insights of quantum mechanics, which will no doubt themselves be eventually superseded in part by new understandings.

Nevertheless, some pictures, proposals and imaginings about the universe have been discarded completely, although for generations they seemed secure and necessary. Spissitude, phlogiston, caloric and aether were all in their time believed to have real existence. They were thought necessary, in order to explain processes such as combustion and the propagation of light. Yet all of them have had to be rejected as non-existent: the unfamiliarity of these terms today shows how completely they have been abandoned. The provisionality and incompleteness of scientific accounts might seem to imply that we can never be sure that anything is either true or false. But to recognise incompleteness does not mean that all things become possible. Some theories, like that of a flat earth, have become simply wrong. We cannot be completely right, but we can be completely wrong. Thus we live, constructively, at the end of well-winnowed and highly reliable traditions, incorporating the wisdom of the past, while at the same time transcending them. As John of Salisbury reported: 'Bernard of Chartres used to say that we, like dwarfs on the shoulders of giants, can see more and farther, not because we are keener and taller, but because of the greatness by which we are carried and exalted.'

THEOLOGY AND THE IMAGINING OF GOD

Science, then, for all its apparently massive assurance and reliability, is nevertheless corrigible and incomplete. Is theology in a similar case? Of course one cannot easily argue from one to the other. God is not an object like a universe; still less is he an object in a universe, to be explored and investigated by apparatus and experiments. Yet it is only through the mediation of our concepts that we can have any apprehension of God. This does not mean that God has no reality apart from our concepts, and that he depends for his existence or his nature on our having opinions concerning him or concepts of him. For the believer God is real, and it is his reality which sets limits to the range of language we can use about him – just as for the scientist the universe is real, and its reality is constantly testing and calling into question the concepts we use to describe it. But all concepts, pictures and imaginings about God, as about anything else, are necessarily incomplete, provisional, approximate and corrigible.

Equally, however, there is no need to conclude from this that theology has nothing to say at all. Theology inherits the long and well-winnowed experience of women and men that there is One who makes a demand upon them which is more like the demand of a person than of an impersonal object, someone to whom they respond in awe, worship, love, prayer, contemplation, adoration, and by acting in the world in ways that have that Someone as their deepest and most abiding resource. Because that demand is an objective reality, it issues in revelation, particularly in the sense that, through the effect of the divine demand on others, God speaks to us. This divine Word is mediated through the circumstances, concepts, lives and actions of God's own creation, and therefore requires interpretation. It is nevertheless identifiable as an objective divine demand upon us, not an invention of our own; and in its relation to particular circumstances and centuries it can properly be spoken of as final. It cannot be remodelled, over and over again, though its implications can certainly be made manifest in as many lives as take it seriously. Revelation enables us to speak reliably and with confidence of God, because he first 'has spoken in times past to our fathers by the prophets, and in these latter days has spoken to us by a Son'.

Yet even here – and perhaps most of all here, in relation to revelation and Scripture – we need to remember that no language, not even the language of Scripture, can supply a complete, final and exhaustive description of what God is, in his own nature. That is why all accounts of God, in all religions, end up, sooner or later, saying of God, 'not this, not this': the *via negativa* of Christianity; the *En Sof* of Judaism; the *bila kaif* of Islam; the *ik onkar* of Sikhism; the *neti, neti* of Hinduism.

In this limited sense, there is a resemblance between our response to the universe and our response to God. What we take to be the universe makes demands upon us in particular and consistent ways, to which we can respond, if we choose to, in appropriate ways. What we take to be God makes its demands upon us likewise in particular and consistent ways, to which again we can respond, if we wish to, in the ways appropriate. 'We love because he loved us first': how we discern that reality, and what we do about it, is what much of this Report is about.

So Christian languages and pictures and imaginings of God have emerged as a consequence not only of revelation, but also of the histories of innumerable individuals and social groups, in which those expressions of belief have been tested, shared, corrected, extended and enhanced. They remain, and always will remain, provisional, corrigible, incomplete and approximate. But they may also be highly reliable. Like scientific traditions, they too have been well-winnowed through time, by women and men who have lived with God as one in whom they have put their trust; and they have not been confounded.

If all pictures and imaginings, even of something as relatively obvious as the observable universe, are necessarily incomplete and corrigible, there is no reason to be upset or alarmed if the same is true in theology. Since God, to be God, must be beyond complete description or precise definition, any representation of God by theology which appeared to be complete and accurate would inevitably be an idol and not God. What theologians offer are much more like scientific 'models' than literal descriptions.

Scientists work with 'models' of what they believe to be real, in order to help their understanding and exploration. But the term 'model' is not used in science in its everyday sense. In ordinary usage a model is a visible reproduction of some real object on a different scale: either smaller, like a toy train or an architect's model of a building, or larger, like the complex models of molecules in a chemistry laboratory. Such models are representations either of what can be observed or of what might be observed, given the technical capacity to do so.

Scientific 'models', however, are not visual representations – not even diagrammatic ones, like a map of the London Underground. They are procedures for enabling us to think about the unobservable. In cosmology, for example, we can imagine a form for the whole cosmos, provide it with a mathematical description, and then see how it might evolve. In theoretical science models are used to investigate hitherto unknown realities not by creating a possible representation of their form, as an ordinary model or a map might do, but by formulating a pattern of their behaviour. Models in this sense are an indispensable tool of scientific thinking.

There are here suggestive clues to the nature of theological thinking. God too is a reality that cannot be observed: 'no one has seen God at any time'. In the classic theological dictum, however, 'God is known by his acts'. As we have stressed from the start in this Report, it is from human experience that theology begins. It is through the created order, through signs or words, or through our relations to ourselves, our neighbours, and the circumstances of time and space in which we live that the presence of God is normally mediated. Theology, with its concepts and images, is not unlike science with its models, in that theology too seeks to explore the unknown and unobservable not by representations but by formulations of the divine behaviour which can then be constantly checked against experience. These theological models, whether boldly pictorial or philosophically abstract, are creative precisely because they are not literal descriptions. They are tools to enable us to think and imagine, and so to advance in our approach to truth. There is a pregnant parallel in something Clerk Maxwell once wrote about science: 'Scientific truth should be presented in different forms, and should be regarded as equally scientific whether it appears in the robust form and vivid colouring of a physical illustration, or in the tenuity and paleness of a symbolic expression.'

FAITH AND CERTAINTY

All this may seem remote from believing in God. But there are five important implications in what has been argued so far. First, all these questions (and all the other ones set down at the beginning of this chapter) remain vital and worth grappling with, only because that to which we give the name of 'God' makes its approach of love towards us. There is rarely any experience of God which is not at the same time experience of something else; and much of this Report is about how we discern the points at which the presence of God is unmistakable. What has been emphasised in this chapter is that Christian communities in the modern world are the end-term (so far) of long and well-winnowed traditions. In ways described in our earlier report, *Believing in the Church*, the traditions protect, and make available to new generations, those points of discernment and connection with God that already anticipate, here and now, what in God's mercy will be our final condition.

Secondly, we have also tried to make clear that it is impossible to give any complete, final and exhaustive account of God, but rather that all accounts must be approximate and incomplete, even while, at the same time, being established as reliable through the winnowing process. This apparent paradox means that all theological pictures, propositions and imaginings carry with them the possibility of being found to be defective or even wrong. We should not be surprised or alarmed that this is so. Some of the pictures of God that have been imagined in the past may come to be discarded, even though, like the scientific pictures of caloric and the aether, they have long seemed to be realistic and have served many generations faithfully as ways of inter-acting with God. We no longer believe, for example, that God is correctly described as a being seated on a celestial throne who regularly consigns large numbers of human beings to a place of torment somewhere below the earth, any more than we believe that creation is correctly described as an event which began at 6 o'clock in the evening of 22nd October in the year 4004 BC and took 144 hours to complete.

The ways in which particular scientific models or religious images are displaced and falsified are by no means simple in either case. It is certainly far beyond the scope of this Report to explore how it happens. But what is true in both cases is that where a model is displaced and agreed to be wrong, it is still possible and necessary to ask, wrong about what? What is it that has set a limit on our language and made us realise that we cannot any longer speak in a particular way? The collapse of a particular picture of God does not mean that 'God has died' – indeed, exactly the reverse. It is precisely because we can know reliably (in the ways already alluded to and discussed much further in other parts of this Report) that God is indeed making his continuing demand upon us, that we realise that some pictures *must* collapse: they are no longer adequate either to present experience or to the implications of the long and continuing traditions which represent the sifting of our knowledge of God and of his dealings with ourselves.

But, thirdly, it is important to remember the advice of Clerk Maxwell and to be generous in our use of images and pictures and symbols (within the constraints of the traditions which have enabled us to speak at all). We should not hesitate to use deeply traditional images in hymns, poetry, liturgy and art, as well as evolving new ones. But at the same time we do not suppose that the sign is identical with what it signifies. Any one of those images is limitless in what it can bring us to be and to understand and to do, as we live with it as an expression of God's relation to us, and of ours to him. Such pictures reinforce and supplement each other, and none can capture the whole reality of God.

This leads to a fourth implication. The fact that those who lived in the past may have held to certain pictures or imaginations which we now know to be defective or even wrong does not mean that they were therefore wholly wrong about everything, nor that they have nothing of value, or of judgement on us, to offer. Newton was not wholly discarded by Einstein. Indeed, Einstein addressed a famous letter to Newton (in his *Autobiographical Notes*) in which, having pointed out why Newton's physics would no longer work for all phenomena, he suddenly pulled himself up and wrote:

Enough of this. Newton, forgive me. You found the only way that, in your day, was at all possible for a man of the highest powers of intellect and creativity. The concepts that you created still dominate the way we think in physics, although we now know that they must be replaced by others farther removed from the sphere of immediate experience if we want to try for a more profound understanding of the way things are interrelated.

Christians too have their own comparable conversation with the past. We live in the Body of Christ and therefore in the communion of saints. We too can recognise that others have left a mark upon us by the prayers they have prayed, by the love they have expressed in life, by the failures for which they have needed forgiveness and have found it. This is to recognise a truth and an experience which we can trust, and on which we are entitled to rely – not uncritically, not as though it foreclosed every argument and solved every problem, but as a great foundation on which to live now for our time and in our day. It is an accumulation, to revert to the earlier language, of irreversible gains.

Finally, it is an implication of all that has been argued here that we should learn to live with the approximate, incomplete and corrigible nature of our languages, not as a defect, but as an asset. It means that where we make judgements (as we must, since traditions of human wisdoms are winnowed, and we have our part to play in that winnowing) we must make them with immense sensitivity, extending even further Chesterton's definition of charity as a reverent agnosticism about the complexity of the human soul. It is also imperative (an imperative derived from the approximate nature of languages) that we do not speak or act towards others as though only our way of speaking, our way of imagining, is valid, to the exclusion of any other.

It follows that although there are judgements of truth and propriety to be made between and within churches (and the report *Believing in the Church* explored how and why these have to be made), we must nevertheless expect that there will be many different ways of living as Christians, both as individuals and as parts of the Church. But in this context, of the provisional and approximate nature of our languages (in which there is immense reliability but no absolute and complete account to the exclusion of all others), we can see that we need these differences to complement and reinforce each other – to realise, in fact, the Pauline picture of the body of Christ, which requires the difference of its members in order to be a body.

Where, then, is the unity? If the Church (as opposed to the churches) is to become fully itself, it will not do so by attempting to achieve a doctrinal definition to which all can assent, for some would always be unable to assent and would then risk being 'unchurched'. It can do so only by realising that our approximate languages (including those of doctrine) are approximate in relation to God, in whom, and in relation to whom, our unity already exists. If all our languages about God are incomplete, then we need each other, precisely in our diversity, to make those languages somewhat less incomplete – or to put it more positively, to enrich and strengthen the ways in which we give glory to God and service to our fellow human beings. That we then have far to go in making practical our connection with each other is obvious. But the ecumenical quest is clearly helped, not hindered, when we recognise that, as a consequence of the incompleteness of our languages, there are bound to be different ways and different styles of being Christian; and that being a Christian in one style is not necessarily betraying, or letting down, Christians who live in another.

What does betray us all is when the impression is given or asserted that all human judgements are so provisional and uncertain that we cannot rely on anything. That is a perversion of the truth. It is certainly the case, to take an example, that historical judgements are incomplete and provisional; and it is therefore legitimate to raise questions about the historicity of the Bible, or of the accounts which are offered there of Jesus. But it is quite illegitimate to draw the conclusion that it offers no basis for historical knowledge at all. That Jesus lived in Galilee and was crucified under Pontius Pilate (to take only two obvious examples) are facts at least as well attested as any others in the history of the ancient world. Of course it is true that historical judgements are provisional, incomplete and corrigible; but it does not follow that they cannot attain a high degree of reliability. Like all historical documents, the New Testament writings may not provide absolute certainty on any particular point; but it would be absurd to suppose that the historical credentials of Christianity are for that reason unreliable.

The distinction is clear: 'God' is not a word or set of images which we use as part of our approximate attempts to describe something else – some way of experiencing the universe or the depth of our relations with each other. Rather, what God truly is, is what constrains and sets a limit on our approximate language about him – just as what is, in the case of the universe, constrains and sets a limit on our approximate (and quite different) language about that. In neither case can those languages be descriptively complete. But the life and experience of people, on which theology depends, make it clear that although in our present condition we see through a glass darkly, we do at least begin to see; and it establishes reliably the belief that what shall be in the end will not end, but will make complete what is here known only in part.

3

God, Language and Personality

Thomas Traherne remarks of a saintly friend that 'he was as familiar with the ways of God in all ages as with his walk and table'. The existence of lives devoted to God cannot be denied, and seems sometimes to speak so powerfully that nothing further needs to be said. But, as already mentioned, there are ways of understanding the world and man's place in it which seem to call in question the assumptions which underlie that devotion. To understand what is implied by belief in God as Creator and Redeemer, and to live that belief effectively, means relating it as fully as possible to what human beings have been able to learn about the world and about themselves – or, since so many of these things are controversial, what they believe themselves to have learnt. Traherne's friend thought similarly for, as Traherne reports, he urged the mature Christian to study philosophy, which in the seventeenth century would have included science.

The attention given to science in the previous chapter is due, chiefly, to the impact science has had upon all aspects of modern life. It has affected the entire context of modern thought in such a way as to influence those who deliberately resist it as well as those who unreservedly welcome it. Once the influence has been recognised it is necessary to respond to it critically and creatively, otherwise there is a risk of being affected more by scientific myths than by scientific facts.

MISLEADING ASSUMPTIONS ABOUT LANGUAGE

The effects of science have been felt not least in the realm of language. It has become common to assume that there are only two ways of using language. One is a literal, fact-stating use, which alone 'conveys information' about the way things are. This is the language of science and of commonsense (thought of as rudimentary science). The other is mood-expressing, attitude-evoking language which is the domain of metaphor and myth and is not designed to carry truth: it is the language of poetry and as such 'subjective', while the other, the language of science, is 'objective'. The assumption is now deeply embedded in our culture that what is scientifically testable is the sole criterion of what is real. Hence the claims of religion are often either rejected altogether as failing the scientific test, or regarded as imaginative constructions which can have value only so long as they do not pretend to truth. Atheists generally take the former view, sympathetic humanists the latter. There are, indeed, some theologians of a radical temper who accept the humanists' analysis and differ from them only in their assessment of the importance of religion, so understood. They are convinced that the attitude to life which, in their view, it is the function of Christian tradition to express is of unique significance and can best be preserved for future generations through the institution of the Church, if only it can be freed from the obsolete metaphysics of traditional theism.

By way of reaction to such tendencies, and subtly affected by them, is a strongly conservative movement which is, for the most part, resolutely anti-critical and prepared, if need be, to maintain the literal truth of the Bible against the claims of modern science. Rightly unwilling to relinquish the conviction that religion deals with matters of fact, and deeply influenced by popular scientific culture in its conception of what facts must be like, it tends to give doctrine a quasi-scientific status and to interpret the biblical writings, wherever possible, as conveying a straightforward record of historical events.

Associated with this dichotomy between factual and expressive language is another – that between public and private domains. It is tempting, in the intellectual climate just described, to draw a distinction between an area of public truth, determined by objective methods of a broadly scientific kind, and a sphere of private preference, where the only sort of truth that obtains is what is 'true for me' or 'true for you'. Religion, it is widely felt, belongs to the latter realm. It is an essentially private matter to do with individuals and their personal feelings. This notion reinforces the conviction many people have that religion has no part to play in the corporate life of a society. Thus the age-old debate about the proper relationship between the sacred and the secular, which has nothing essentially to do with this distinction, is, in contemporary discussion, often infected by it.

THE LANGUAGE OF SCIENCE

Such is the distorting effect of this assumption about the use of language upon the general understanding of religious truth that it is vital to examine its credentials. Do scientists deal in bare descriptive statements? Have poets no concern with truth? It has already been shown (chapter 2) that the nature of scientific knowledge is very much more complex than such simple contrasts would suggest. People who are alarmed at what they see as the iconoclastic tendencies of some contemporary theologians might be surprised at some recent discussions among philosophers and sociologists of science. There are, for example, those who maintain that the theories, models and equations of scientists are nothing but 'social constructions of reality', and give us no access to what that reality is like independently of ourselves. Far from providing the paradigm case of publicly accessible objective knowledge, science is regarded by these thinkers as a cultural creation of vast imaginative power which reflects human concerns rather than the structure of the universe.

Such views, like their theological counterparts, may be exaggerated. But they do serve to correct the naive assumption that science provides us with an unproblematically factual description of the universe which, once achieved, remains for ever beyond question. It is now widely accepted that that naive view requires correction in two important ways. One is that, rather than just observing what is there, scientists devise provisional models of the reality they are trying to understand, and test these models by drawing out their implications and discovering by experiment in what respects they hold and in what respects they do not. The capacity to find appropriate models is an essential element in the make-up of creative scientists, and has much in common with other uses of the imagination. It has in the past been one of the failures of the educational system that the teaching of science has rarely communicated any appreciation of the scientist's creative and exploratory role, and has too often been content to hand on the findings of science as so much cut and dried information.

The other way in which the naive view of science has to be modified is in the recognition that, as the models employed in a particular science are repeatedly qualified and reshaped, the resulting body of theory becomes an increasingly reliable set of 'representations' of reality. Thus, as was argued in the last chapter, the sciences become 'well-winnowed' traditions of great reliability, although they always remain provisional, corrigible and incomplete.

THE LANGUAGE OF POETRY

If the dichotomy between the objective fact-stating and the subjective mood-expressing uses of language is misleading about science, it is equally misleading about poetry. Poetry does, of course, express emotion, but to suggest that this is all it does is to suppose that emotions are bare feelings, directed upon the environment quite independently of one's beliefs about it. There are, doubtless, moods which colour for the time being one's perception of the world, so that the poet who describes the world as seen in this mood is felt to be conveying the mood rather than some truth about the world as it 'really is'.

> Out, out, brief candle!
> Life's but a walking shadow, a poor player,
> That struts and frets his hour upon the stage,
> And then is heard no more; it is a tale
> Told by an idiot . . .

But even in such a case Macbeth, in his despair, gives expression to a vision of life which challenges us as to its truth: is this how things really are? It would be a shallow interpretation of Macbeth's utterance to regard it simply as a memorable expression of a certain mood that a man might have, that was understandable in the circumstances, etc. The mood itself is similar in

> As flies to wanton boys, are we to the gods;
> They kill us for their sport

but a different, more explicitly pessimistic philosophy is conveyed, recognisably the same as that expressed in Thomas Hardy's final word on Tess of the D'Urbervilles:

> The President of the Immortals (in Aeschylean phrase) had ended his sport with Tess.

It is not to be supposed that poets always claim truth, or at any rate ultimate truth, for what they write, especially when it is put into the mouth of a dramatic character. The dramatist presents a vision of the world as it seems to a given character in a given situation. To that extent he himself is, as it were, at two removes from reality. Yet the drama would not move us if the characters did not engage with the common world and try to make sense of it as we do. So through them he offers us something which might be true, which is, so to speak, a candidate for truth; and as such engages our emotions and solicits our commitment. We can scarcely be indifferent to it. Sometimes there is no doubt that the poet in his own person shares the commitment to which he gives expression, sometimes there may be reason to think he does not. To the literary critic in either case it may not matter. But the world could be as the poet represents it, and if it were, certain feelings would be appropriate, certain decisions justified. The relationship between the poet as uncommitted and the poet as committed (or anyone else who uses the poet's words to

express his own commitment) is something like that
between a mathematician and a physicist in relation to
mathematical models. The mathematician devises models
which could, in principle, apply to some physical reality,
without himself trying to decide whether they do or not.
The physicist is primarily concerned with just this
question.

Hence, when Shakespeare defines the character of love,
it is recognisably the Christian *agape* that he has in mind:

> . . . Love is not love
> Which alters when it alteration finds,
> Or bends with the remover to remove:
> O, no! it is an ever-fixed mark,
> That looks on tempests and is never shaken;
> It is the star to every wandering bark,
> Whose worth's unknown, although his height be taken.
> Love's not Time's fool . . .

The reader is invited, no doubt, to share the poet's
admiration of the quality he sets forth, but the purpose of
his cumulation of images is to make precise what it is that
we are to admire: a love that offers us safety in a storm,
serenely guides us, is not at the mercy of Time. The
strength of the poet's own commitment is evinced by the
final couplet:

> If this be error, and upon me prov'd,
> I never writ, nor no man ever lov'd.

It is upon the truth of his utterances that he stakes himself.

The notion that the poet, by contrast with the scientist,
is concerned only to express emotion, in such a way that
no question of truth arises, will not stand examination.
Unlike the scientist he is not, as a rule, concerned to
generalise and analyse, but rather to describe what is
individual and unique, whether it be an abstract idea or a
particular thing. In either case the use of comparisons both
extends the scope of possible understanding and brings
what is described into clearer focus. The reader's imagination is led on to analogies not yet thought of, while at the
same time being constrained by the variety of the images
to conceive of the subject with greater precision, in a way

that is consistent with them all. Hence Austin Farrer writes:

> The poet is a man who has a gift for grasping fresh and profound resemblances, and that is why he works with metaphor, and why his metaphors illuminate the nature of things. This gift can only work by inspiration (*Reflective Faith*, p. 32).

The purpose of this discussion of scientific and poetic discourse has been to dispel a pervasive assumption which makes it impossible for some people today to entertain the thought of God at all except as an aspect of human subjectivity, and which encourages others, by an understandable reaction, to construe religious doctrines with unqualified literalness. Neither scientific nor poetic language conforms to the required stereotype. It seems, instead, to be a basic propensity of the human mind to extend its knowledge by the use of the imagination, endeavouring to form images or models of the way things might be, and then testing the hypothesis in the appropriate manner. The reason why metaphor plays the part it does in scientific discourse is precisely because it is the equivalent in language of thinking with models.

THE LANGUAGE OF DEVOTION

The language of devotion is, in most respects, closer to the language of poetry than to the language of science. Indeed it often is poetical language put to a religious use. But, as already argued, this does not in the least imply that it makes no claim to truth, or that it cannot achieve precise statement, or that what it claims cannot be tested.

The overlap between devotion and poetry is most familiar to us in hymns, and it is through hymns that most people become familiar with the doctrines of the Church. When John Newton piles image upon image in

> Jesus, my Shepherd, Husband, Friend,
> My Prophet, Priest and King,
> My Lord, my Life, my Way, my End,
> Accept the praise I bring

he is employing metaphors well known to him from the Bible where, as George Caird remarks,

> The five metaphors in most common use to express God's relationship with his worshippers are King/subject, judge/litigant, husband/wife, father/child, master/servant (*The Language and Imagery of the Bible*, p. 177).

The metaphors used are, in these instances, all anthropomorphic and it is obvious that there are dangers attaching to this. To many of these dangers the biblical writers were, as Caird points out, alert:

> God is not, like mankind, subject to vacillation and weakness (1 Sam. 15:29; Isa. 55:8; Hos. 11:9; Mal. 3:6). Human judges may be corruptible (1 Sam. 8:3), but it is axiomatic that the judge of all the earth shall do right (Gen. 18:25). Human parents may falter in love for their children, but God's love does not fail (Isa. 49:15). Israel's loyalty disperses like a morning mist (Hos. 6:4), but God's loyalty is everlasting (Ps. 100:5) (*ibid.*, pp. 175-6).

To some extent the dangers are lessened by the use, as a counterweight, of impersonal metaphors which there is little or no temptation to take literally. God is a sun, a rock, a tower, a devouring fire. Not only do these qualify the personal metaphors, and reduce the risk of misreading them, but they are more effective in conveying God's eternity, independence and awfulness.

But even when allowance has been made for the extent to which the various metaphors modify one another, there remains the question how to know which features of all of them are to be disallowed – as some must be when one is speaking of God. When the poet says of a girl,

> O, my love's like a red, red rose
> That's newly sprung in June.
> O, my love's like the melodie
> That's sweetly played in tune

we know enough about girls from common observation to tell that the poet is not taking her to be some sort of plant. We know, similarly, that if a preacher refers to 'the hand of the Lord', or if a hand pointing down from heaven appears in a medieval carving, God is not being presented as actually having a hand. God is not, in any ordinary sense, embodied. The biblical writers, when they stressed the limitations of the metaphors they used of God, relied upon some knowledge of him which was not derived from these metaphors alone and which was able to some extent to control their use. This creates a problem which is sometimes presented as a dilemma: either it is possible to make straightforwardly literal statements about God or all language about him is symbolic. In the latter case we seem, as it were, to be trapped in a circle of images, from which there is no escape. Unable to observe God directly (as we can the girl), we have no means of knowing whether, as it were, our images catch his likeness. But the former alternative is equally impossible. If God is, as he must be, transcendent, how can one say things about him that are literally true, using language in just the same sense as it is used about human beings?

This, however, is not a genuine dilemma. When models are used in science (as mentioned in chapter 2), the appropriateness of the model as a source of information about the real world is demonstrated not by direct observation of the electron itself, the results of which are then compared with the model, but by working out the implications of the model and testing them by experiment. Again, for it to be possible to use some words literally about God, it is not necessary that they should be used in just the same sense as when used about human beings. Personal language can be used about God without its carrying all the implications that such language has when used of ourselves.

People often fail to see this because they tend to regard as figurative any language which is not employed in precisely the same sense as it is when talking about the ordinary world of things and people. So not only is 'the hand of the Lord' treated as metaphorical, or 'The Lord is my shepherd', but also any talk of God as all-knowing, faithful or loving. All such languge is then liable to be dismissed as 'mere metaphor'.

But when Charles Wesley writes of 'love divine all loves excelling' he is not using human love as a 'metaphor' for divine love, but stretching the use of 'love' in its human context to represent the perfect love of God, to which love as we know it is only an approximation. Hence Bishop Berkeley distinguished between 'metaphorical' and 'proper' analogy:

> By metaphorical analogy God is represented as having a finger or an eye, as angry or grieved: by proper analogy we must understand all those properties to belong to the deity which, in themselves, simply and as such denote perfection.

Thus, he says, 'It is a mistake to say we can never have any direct or proper notion of knowledge or wisdom as they are in the deity.' Knowledge and wisdom are, indeed, personal attributes, as are love, mercy, forgiveness, faithfulness. All of these are normally encountered in human beings, but all of them can also be conceived of as freed from the limitations of their expression in human lives. Perhaps also, in spite of what Berkeley says, divine anger and divine grief may also be so conceived. (This will be one of the questions discussed in chapter 10.)

THE LANGUAGE OF DEVOTION AND THE LANGUAGE OF METAPHYSICS

In the light of this discussion it will be seen that the use of metaphors in thinking about God is controlled, not only by the interaction between the metaphors themselves, but also by theism as a metaphysical theory. There is here some analogy to the way in which a physicist may use the apparatus of theory to control his use of models. The metaphors or 'models' used in thinking about God operate within the overall structure of a rational theory that the universe was created by a God who, as William Temple used to put it, is 'at least personal', and whose purposes may be learned in some degree through his creation and through his revelation of himself.

Some people find the whole notion of theory unpalatable in relation to religion because it suggests to them an attitude totally remote from that of worship – as if it implied that the Creator could be known in some quasi-scientific and uncommitted way. The God of the philosophers, they claim with Pascal, has nothing to do with the God of Abraham, Isaac and Jacob. True devotion does not argue to God as personal, but assumes, by the very form of worship, that God is personal. Nor is the worshipper concerned to define God's attributes or to pay him 'metaphysical compliments'.

But, once again, it looks as if this is a case of posing false alternatives. It is true that a philosopher who seeks to develop a rational case for the existence of God is not, in the act of doing so, engaged in worship; but his case, if it is sound, points to a God who must transcend human understanding and is the proper object of worship. And the language of devotion itself often gives poetical expression to metaphysical concepts:

> O Lord, thou hast searched me out and known me: thou knowest my down-sitting and mine up-rising, thou understandest my thoughts long before . . .
> Whither shall I go then from thy Spirit: or whither shall I go then from thy presence?
> If I climb up into heaven, thou art there: if I go down to hell, thou art there also.
> If I take the wings of the morning: and remain in the uttermost parts of the sea;
> Even there also shall thy hand lead me: and thy right hand shall hold me. (Ps. 139.1, 6-9)

Here are many of the 'metaphysical' attributes of God, his transcendence and his omnipresence, his omniscience and his providence. Yet the psalmist is not composing a philosophical argument, but addressing a hymn of thanksgiving: 'I will give thanks unto thee, for I am fearfully and wonderfully made.'

This should not be surprising, for the psalmist is writing superb poetry, and it is, as we have seen, one of the properties of poetry to be able to give memorable expression to a vision of the world by describing through metaphors (and through stretching the ordinary use of language) what in its essential nature can never fully be grasped. It is not the function of the poet, as poet, to assert the truth of what is thus conveyed, nor is it the function of the devotional writer to argue that truth or to analyse it. But it does, nevertheless, need to be argued, and also to be analysed, if its coherence and truth is to be vindicated against its critics.

Poets can give poetical expression to a world-view without declaring their own position. In the same way, philosophers can analyse such a view, develop its implications and examine the arguments for and against it, without declaring theirs. But everyone, whether poet or philosopher or anything else, must choose (or live as if they have chosen) how they are to view the world. This universal human predicament provides the context in which the philosopher and the poet are able to pursue their callings. It is because everyone has come to terms in some way with the limitations of human existence that rival philosophical and religious traditions develop, and it is these traditions which provide the terrain for the intellectual and imaginative explorations of the philosopher and the poet.

So the philosopher who reasons to the existence of a creator who is 'at least personal' and the poet who celebrates the presence of God in creation, whatever their individual stances, depend upon a community in which this belief is lived. The characteristic elements in worship – praise, thanksgiving, intercession, sacrament – in their nature presuppose some kind of personal relationship with God (though the meaning of the word 'personal' is very evidently stretched beyond its everyday uses). If, however, God is rightly thought of as personal, there will be significant analogies between our relationship with God and one with our fellow human beings. Thus, our ordinary dealings with other people not only enable us to stay alive and to realise our own particular purposes, but are essential to our fulfilment as persons, indeed to our becoming persons at all. These purposes depend upon a degree of mutual love and trust; and this means being open and receptive to other people, their hopes and aspirations, intentions and purposes. It follows that awareness of God can no more be purely theoretical than can our awareness of people, but must involve seeking to know and respond to his will. There is need of a continuous devotional experiment, in which those who seek to do the will learn of the doctrine.

GOD AND THE NATURE OF PERSONS

That the religious life has this form of personal interaction is easily recognised, though it manifests itself very differently in different communities and, indeed, in different individuals at different periods of their lives. Traherne's joyful and triumphant celebration in childhood of the presence of God in creation came to him more rarely in later life, and to many others it does not come at all, though they seek to carry out the will of God obediently. But whether marked by experiences of ecstasy or of alienation, of enthusiastic response or of sober dedication, the pattern of such a life presupposes God as its focus. It is for this reason that for many people the most convincing witness to the reality of God is that of those in whose lives his grace is apparent.

But it does not follow that the theory of the matter is unimportant, any more than it is in the case of persons. It is true that the sheer existence of persons is something which it is impossible, while sane, to doubt, since the very language needed to frame such a doubt is, and could only be, the product of a community of persons. By contrast, it is possible to doubt the existence of God. But how we conceive of persons, what we take them to be, affects profoundly the way we are able to understand them and relate to them, and the same must be true of God. For instance, to think of other people exhaustively in terms drawn from our experience of computer-based 'artificial intelligence', is to do away with any sense of their mysteriousness, of creative possibilities which transcend our present horizons; and having left no room for these in our thinking, we render ourselves unable to elicit them or respond to them in practice. If persons are thought of merely as bundles of perceptions linked together by psychological laws, there can be no awareness of their continuous identity through time, of their shaping and being shaped by their experiences, of their role as moral agents responsible for what they have done yesterday and will do tomorrow. Mr Gradgrind in Dickens's *Hard Times* is a caricature, but a salutary one, of what such an attitude can mean in practice. When confronted with this kind of analysis of what it is to be a human being, we feel bound to protest that there is more to people than just this. But protest alone is not enough; it is necessary to argue the case.

The tendency to substitute protest for argument is itself an illustration of the dichotomy from which this chapter started. There is a strong tendency for each of the two sides in the dispute just mentioned to suppose that they need take no notice of what the other says about human personality. Those on the one side claim that the model of artificial intelligence explains the physical and mental phenomena so fully that it can be regarded as having scientific warrant. No doubt a lot more detail needs to be filled in, but that is only a matter of time. If others feel that this leaves only a rather attenuated notion of what it is to be a human being, that is simply evidence of the degree of superstition and ignorance that the traditional idea has carried with it. The depths that have allegedly been left out are depths of illusion merely. Those on the other side 'know' that there is more to people than this model allows and are not to be persuaded otherwise. Like Dr Johnson on a related topic they 'know our will is free and there's an end on't'.

The current debate about the nature of human personality illustrates a further feature of talk about God in personal terms. How we think of people affects and is affected by how we think of God. Only if human beings are themselves thought of as possessing a genuine mystery and creativity can they be taken as images of the divine; and their being so taken helps us to think of them in this way. At first it may seem as if the attributes of God are simply read off from ordinary human understanding of kings, judges, husbands, fathers, and so forth. In the words of the old jest, 'God made man in his own image, and man returned the compliment'. But if the king or the judge is to be the clue to the majesty and justice of God, only the disinterested king and the impartial judge will serve that purpose. Moreover the divine king or judge is also the divine parent who has all human beings as his children, so that the human ruler or judge, who follows that pattern, may not consider only their own subjects or their own fellow countrymen. Similarly Hosea's vision of God's love for Israel as being like a husband's continuing love for an unfaithful wife illuminates both sides of the comparison. Within the whole framework of belief in God the use of personal imagery for God is not to be seen as just a matter of there happening to be resemblances at hand for the religious thinker to use. The resemblances are built by God into the human situation itself:

> What is man, that thou art mindful of him: and the son of man, that thou visitest him?
>
> Thou madest him lower than the angels: to crown him with glory and worship.

SOME IMPLICATIONS OF BELIEF IN GOD

It follows that belief in God makes a difference to the way we think about everything else. Nothing of importance is wholly unaffected by it. Thus, men and women have a dignity which comes of their being made in the image of God, so that they cannot be regarded merely as elaborate machines; but neither has humankind the sort of sovereign independence and autonomy which would be needed to make human preferences the final arbiter of morality. Human beings are not free to choose what shall count as human goodness, for this depends upon the purposes of God in creation; nevertheless they are themselves in a genuine, though dependent, way creative and free to decide how they will develop their gifts. Living as rational creatures in a created universe, they have reason to believe that its structure will be in some way congruous with their intellectual powers and that, if they use these rightly, they will come to know it better. They will, therefore, be prepared to trust scientific enquiry as providing a genuine, if always limited, understanding of the cosmos as it is. Fearing idolatry, they will not be willing to accord to anything less than God the devotion owed to God alone, but they will also be aware that God's kingdom cannot be confined to a purely private sphere. Hence, while not investing all their hopes in political programmes, they will seek to maintain and promote the conditions of a free and just society.

If belief in God has such implications as these, a civilisation which has been founded upon it, however incompletely, is bound to suffer severe strains to the extent that this belief is withdrawn. There is much in our situation to suggest that faith in God has, so to speak, been 'drying out' and that we are now experiencing some of the effects of shrinkage. It might be argued that a 'scientific world-view' implies that the only valid mode of reasoning is scientific reasoning, that a scientific account of the universe and of humankind exhausts all that can be known, and that language used in a purely analytical and descriptive manner can say all that can intelligibly be said. But would not such a position, if it were held, end up, after denaturing nature and dehumanising humanity, by destroying its own credentials? For there would be no room left for rationality as a guide to truth. The only means of escape then left is a desperate attempt to rescue humanness by retreating to the only place that science cannot reach, the inner recesses of the individual mind, where all is subjectivity. Here poetry and the other arts, and even religion itself, are constrained to take refuge and, as Iris Murdoch puts it, 'the agent, thin as a needle, appears in the quick flash of the choosing will'. There is no longer any sense of an overarching purpose which gives meaning and coherence to human existence.

There are still many people who would prefer to evade these fundamental issues. Suspicious of intellectual debate, they remain confident that a humane commonsense will continue to take care of moral and political values and of the conception of humanity upon which they have habitually been based, while explicit belief in God can be regarded as an optional extra, privately available. No doubt this unreflective maintenance of generally good habits has its proper place, but the present age is one in which such habits are increasingly hard to sustain in the absence of deliberate decision. Explicit challenges increasingly demand explicit choices.

The starting-point of our argument was the existence, as an acknowledged fact, of religious devotion in its many manifestations, individual and corporate. This led to a consideration of the way in which belief in God is expressed in language and given an intellectual structure; how it is related to our understanding of the world and of humankind, as derived from the sciences, the humanities and the arts; how it unifies the emotions and directs the wills of those who accept it, or have been influenced by it, whether they consciously accept it or not.

The question remains, is it true? And how are we to tell if it is true? It is reasonable to believe that something is true if it sorts better with our individual and corporate experience of life than do the alternatives to it; if to deny it would compel us to reject along with it too much of what we otherwise have reason to believe; if to do so would force us to repudiate our deepest intuitions when they have been critically considered; if it turns out that, when we try to live by it, we find our path illuminated, not completely, but enough to take us forward step by step; if our faith is reinforced by that of others, when we have exerted our imaginations to appropriate it.

Such a test is possible. But to make it we need more than just our own individual resources of thought and experience. As described in the preceding chapter, we depend upon developed traditions which nevertheless, if they are to remain alive, require that we respond to them openly, critically and creatively. The next section, therefore, turns to look at the Church's traditions in this matter by tracing the history of the Christian understanding of God.

4

The God of the Bible

We referred at the outset to three factors in the search for a doctrine of God: revelation, reason and experience. It is time to return to the first of these – the truth that is revealed to us in Holy Scripture. Even if, as was said earlier, Scripture is not such that an agreed doctrine of God can be deduced from it, does it not provide the indispensable data on which reason can get to work and by which all subsequent experience of God must be assessed?

For reasons which were discussed at some length in *Believing in the Church*,[1] Scripture does occupy a uniquely authoritative position among the available sources of belief. But it can be misleading to talk as if this necessarily sets Scripture over against reason and experience. Reason can indeed get to work on Scripture, but is it not already at work in Scripture? Subsequent experience may be subject to the control of Scripture, but did not a wide range of experience contribute to its formation?

THE ORIGINS OF SCRIPTURE

We may start from the most obvious point about Scripture: that (as its name implies) it is written. Moreover it is written for the most part in forms which are recognisably literary: poetry, narrative, letters and so forth. These forms seem to presuppose in each case an individual author; and it should therefore be possible to ask how these authors were enabled to write in such a way that

---

[1] pp. 30 ff.

their work continues to carry authority among believers. How did they get their information about and their insight into God's character and workings and their ability to communicate these to so many generations and in infinitely varied cultures? This is the question to which the Church has tried to respond with its doctrine of Inspiration. In *Believing in the Church*[2] some account was given of the difficulties involved in this enterprise. Explanations have ranged from direct divine dictation given to the writer to a general control exerted by divine providence over the events and circumstances leading up to the writing. It is probably true to say that none of the traditional answers proposed to the question of inspiration has proved entirely satisfactory; and one of the reasons for this may be that each of them has worked with the presupposition of an individual author responsible for each book of the Bible. The question has consequently tended to present itself in personal, even psychological, terms: what were the circumstances, and what was the mental state, in which it was possible for the writer to have such privileged access to divine truth?

It is true, of course, that certain books of the Bible are undoubtedly the work of individual authors, some of whom are known by name. Even if subsequent editors have introduced alterations or additions to the text soon after it was composed, there can be no doubt that most of the letters attributed to St Paul are the authentic work of the writer himself. In the Old Testament a book like Ecclesiastes bears the unmistakable stamp (apart, again, from certain additions) of the mind of an individual author. But, taking the Bible as a whole, these instances are the exception rather than the rule. It is not just that we do not happen to know for certain who wrote the book of Genesis or the histories of Samuel and the Kings or the Fourth Gospel; it is rather that the question itself does not seem altogether pertinent. Many books of the Bible seem deliberately anonymous. The consensus of mainstream

[2] pp. 34–36.

scholarship has long since ceased to be that Moses was the single author of the first five books of the Bible or that all the Psalms were composed by King David; and from earliest times Christians have been in doubt about the identity of the writers of some, if not all, of the Gospels. Moreover there can be no doubt that in the case of the Gospels (as a number of Old Testament books) a period of 'oral tradition' must have preceded the actual moment of writing. Sayings of Jesus, and episodes of his life story, were preserved and communicated by word of mouth, just as local stories and traditions are still preserved in 'folk memory', though there was probably a greater capacity for accurate memory in the time of Jesus than is normally possessed by people today. Clearly the authority of many, if not most, biblical writings does not depend on the authority of any individual writer; and to discuss how the presumed writer came to write as he did may be to misconceive the nature of the writing itself.

One of the most significant contributions of modern critical scholarship has been to develop this simple observation and to reconstruct the processes by which this unique literature came into being. Behind all the scholarly discussions of sources, oral tradition and literary forms lies the recognition, confirmed again and again by study of the text, that these writings are the product, not simply of individual authors, but also of communities. Even the highly individual utterances of an Isaiah or a Jeremiah have come down to us in a form heavily worked over by a 'school' of prophetic writers. The legal and historical material of the Old Testament was shaped by centuries of community experience and reflection. A collection of liturgical poetry such as the Psalter is an anthology of poems (even if originally by individual authors) used and adapted by a people in their worship. The Gospels themselves are the end-product of a period of several decades, during which information about Jesus was recalled, shared and preserved by the growing Christian churches. It can never have been true to the nature of Scripture to regard it solely as the medium through which a succession of uniquely inspired writers has conveyed the truth about God to later generations, even though such writers, named or unnamed, must have played a crucial part. Scripture is also, and perhaps chiefly, the distillation of those perceptions of the reality of God which came to a worshipping community under the impact of particular historical events, of the genius of legislators, prophets and thinkers, and finally of the encounter with Jesus himself. This in turn tells us something of immense importance about God: that God is known, primarily and characteristically, in the shared worship, experience and reflection of men and women who meet in his name and serve him in the world. What we have observed in the human apprehension of God in our own time is also reflected in Scripture itself, and is authenticated by it.

THE BIBLE AS NARRATIVE

There is another general feature which is characteristic of a great deal of the Bible and which may suggest something quite specific about God. This feature often seems to present something of a problem. If the Bible is read in order to discover what God is like, it is reasonable to look for statements describing his nature and attributes. But in fact the characteristic way in which the Bible communicates its ideas is not by doctrinal statements, nor by creeds or catechisms or summaries of the faith, but by narratives or stories. More than half of both Testaments consists of lengthy accounts of 'what happened', either in the ancient history of Israel or in the life of Jesus and of the early church. Anyone who attends a service where there are readings from the Bible is practically certain to hear some part of this narrative read; and such a person may well wonder therefore how Christians move from the Bible, with its great emphasis on 'telling the story', to doctrine, in the sense of an ordered body of beliefs about God and the world.

It is true that in many of these stories God himself is said to be acting or speaking; and conclusions can therefore be drawn from them about the nature and purposes of God. But in others the implied doctrine is less easy to discern. Sometimes the story read seems positively unedifying (for example, some of the stories in the book of Judges); but even where there is nothing at all offensive in the story, it may be difficult to see in what sense it can be the basis for doctrine. Stories are stories, not doctrinal formularies. Even if we believe that every story in the Bible is literally true, something more is needed to help us move from reading the stories to formulating doctrine about God.

In one sense it is true that a story conveys less about God than does a statement of doctrine. It does not define what God is like; it may not be completely clear with which of the actors in the story God aligns himself. Indeed stories are often morally ambiguous, and yield differing impressions of each character which are not always fully consistent with each other. Besides this, a story is always about particular incidents, not universal truths, and its 'moral', or meaning, may be impossible to express without remainder in a series of general propositions. But in another, perhaps more important, sense, stories can reveal more than doctrines. The very fact that a story is always particular means that it is prevented from degenerating into a mere idea or set of platitudes. The biblical stories in particular are very concrete, and present human experiences that we can set alongside our own. We are not simply told that God is loving, or merciful, or just, or demanding: we are shown these things in action.

To say that God is revealed ir story in the Bible is to say something, not just about the Bible, but about God himself. It is a clue to the power of God to influence the human heart. Few people are led to belief in God or to an understanding of his ways by reading books of speculative theology, but many owe their faith in good measure to stories – not only the stories of the Bible, but the stories told by novelists and poets and perhaps above all the stories told by their friends. What is the 'testimony' which to many Christians is so significant if not one person's story of his or her own life, interpreted in the light of faith, and challenging the hearer, 'This happened to me; it can also happen to you'?

The God, then, in whom we believe is one about whom it is appropriate to speak by means of narrative. To this extent at least, God is personal. In Pascal's phrase, he is not the God of the philosophers, but the God of Abraham, Isaac and Jacob. He is a God who, like other persons, is often best described by presenting him within a narrative of events. But not any narrative. Certain things must be the case about the narrative if it is to speak of God. It must, in the first place, have a certain shape. The stories in the Bible, and the overall single story to which they all contribute, is a coherent and purposeful story. The biblical story is not vague, or rambling, or inconsequential; it is sharply focused and it makes overall sense. Indeed, if we are uncomfortable with the Bible it is probably in part because its strongly unitary thrust tends to threaten us with a view of human history that is too tightly organised, too coherent, to fit the ambiguities of the world as we in modern times perceive them. For the modern reader, the problem of the Bible is not that it does not hang together but rather that it seems to hang together almost too well, to make sense of chains of events that strike us as much more aimless than the biblical writers let them be. It is difficult to recognise our world in the schematised history of the books of Kings, where the kings of Israel and Judah are simply 'good' and 'bad', or in the church as described in Acts, where people are either saints or renegades. But it is important to set this feeling in context, and to realise that the biblical stories are a monument to a faith which tried to see a coherent divine purpose in events which many contemporaries would have regarded as quite random and meaningless. For both Jewish and Christian tradition faith in God is faith that his people's history does have a proper story-line, that it is not merely a succession of unrelated and futile incidents. To read in worship any portion of the biblical story – however truncated or broken it may seem taken alone – is to set our own lives in the context of the whole narrative framework which the Bible contains.

Over and above the particular truths about God that some of the stories may contain, their existence as parts of one long and complete story carries a great additional weight of meaning; for it affirms that human existence is seen as standing under the purposes of God.

A second thing that may reasonably be asked of any narrative or series of narratives, and all the more in the case of narratives about God, is that the principal character should speak and act consistently and comprehensibly. A story in which the characters appear to behave in a random and unpredictable way can tell us little. If the biblical narrative is to tell us about God it must show him to have reasonably consistent intentions and attitudes. It is here, as we said at the outset, that we run into difficulties. The God of the Bible is described in many ways. Sometimes he is a severe judge who is ready to sentence some of his creatures to eternal punishment, sometimes a loving Father who wills everyone to be saved. The problem is perhaps less acute in the Old Testament, when it can be argued that a particular episode (such as God's command to slaughter the Amalekites) represents a 'primitive' stage in the people's experience. But in the New Testament, where such a solution is not readily available, there is also considerable tension between apparent opposites – between God's implacable wrath on the one hand and his infinite mercy on the other. Christians have tended to react to this tension by emphasising different aspects at different times. Present-day New Testament scholars, for example, tend to stress the evidence which points to an explicit and remarkably intimate father-son relationship with God on the part of Jesus, a relationship subsequently extended into the experience of his followers. The perception of God as devouring fire (Heb. 12.29) and awesome judge is one to which today not only scholars but most Christian people tend to pay less attention. Nor are these isolated instances, which could perhaps be dismissed as the quirks of particular authors. Both perceptions (along with many others) are well represented in the New Testament. At any particular time Christians may feel justified in emphasising one and virtually ignoring the other, but the fact they are both there forbids us from permanently discarding either. Scripture claims that the 'character' of God (if we may speak in this way) is sufficiently consistent for him to be the subject of the narrative or series of narratives it contains; but it also constantly challenges us to enlarge our understanding of that character by postulating a range of attributes that could hardly be held together in the case of a single human being.

Today's emphasis on the mercy, rather than the wrath, of God is only one example of the way in which Christian (as well as Jewish) reflection on the Scriptures tends to stress those aspects which seem most acceptable to a contemporary understanding of God and to neglect others which, though equally clearly attested in Scripture, seem to present too great a challenge to our imagining. Another example is the traditional portrayal of God by means of models or attributes derived from the activities and attitudes of men rather than women. In cultures in which power, authority and education are typically in the hands of men it is inevitable that God should be pictured with predominantly masculine characteristics. Yet here again the Bible offers a wider range of attributes. God is occasionally described in terms of tenderness and long-suffering vigilance usually thought more appropriate to motherhood than fatherhood. Jesus, too, uses imagery of himself (that of a hen gathering her chicks) which points in the same direction. Our own generation, with its concern for the equality and complementarity of the sexes, invites fresh attention to this aspect of the biblical tradition, so that the richness of Scripture's perception of God may enlarge our imagining to press beyond our own restricted models and categories of gender towards the ultimate mystery of God.[1]

A further question raised by the predominantly narrative character of biblical material about God is that of its historical truth. In recent years theologians have used the

---

[1] Cf. *The Motherhood of God* (Church of Scotland), Edinburgh 1984.

word 'myth' in connection with biblical narratives, to indicate that the meaning of the stories in the Bible goes far deeper than the significance of their historical content. They are stories expressing profound insight into the relationship of God, humankind and world. But in ordinary usage the word myth suggests a story that is not true. The myths of Greek gods and heroes, for example, are not for the most part taken as accounts of events that can be located in history. Is it now being suggested that the biblical narrative is equally 'mythical'? The reaction of many has been, once again, to stress the historical character of the biblical revelation. The Christian story, it is urged, is in the strict factual sense 'true'.

It may be that the 'myth' approach was exaggerated; it was certainly widely misunderstood. But the reaction too has sometimes been over-simple. The relationship of the biblical narrative to historical events is a complex one. In the book of Genesis, for example, the narrative moves from legendary and 'mythical' material (the creation of the world in six days, the Flood, the Tower of Babel, etc.), through episodes of 'patriarchal' history which have a real but distant relationship with known movements of tribes and peoples, into the sequence of Joseph-stories, which can be fairly precisely related to known Egyptian background – all without any perceptible change of style or intention. Similarly, two consecutive verses of Mark's gospel (15.37-38) contain the statements that Jesus expired and that the curtain of the Temple was split from top to bottom. The first of these is plainly what we would call a statement of fact. There are good grounds, however, for thinking that the second is not a description of a supernatural or freakish phenomenon but is intended by the evangelist to be a symbolic statement of the significance of Jesus's death. In that case, the two statements stand in totally different relationships to historical truth but once again the biblical text gives us no inkling that it is 'changing gear' at this point.

Although, therefore, there is good reason to believe that the story of God's involvement in the affairs of his people and of the world is firmly rooted in historical fact, we have to recognise that the actual telling of the story, if it is to bring out the significance and implications of this involvement, may depart at times from the strictly factual reporting expected of scientific historians. This again tells us something of importance about God. If he can legitimately be represented as an actor in and influence upon the course of history, the nature of this action and influence is too subtle and varied always to be adequately expressed in objective historical statement. The contribution that is increasingly being made by literary critics to biblical studies, with its emphasis on the different modes of composition and expression found in different parts of the Bible or even of a single text, has helped to illuminate not just Scripture but by implication also the nature of God himself.

BIBLICAL HISTORY AND OTHER HISTORY

This complex relationship of the biblical narrative to history raises the further question: history of whom and of what? If any meaning is to be found in the proposition that the activity and influence of God are to be discerned in historical events, there must be some events in which this is so and some in which it is not. But how are we to distinguish between them? The status of Scripture as the primary source of knowledge about God might seem to settle the question: those events which are recounted in the Bible reveal the intentions and activity of God, others do not – or at least not to the same degree. But as soon as we begin to take seriously the character of these events as real history, it becomes necessary to bring the normal methods of historical study to bear on them. They must be closely related to other events and circumstances not reported in the Bible, and a greater knowledge of these (when it is available) can be expected to increase understanding of the biblical narrative itself. It is this conviction which in modern times has intensified research by biblical scholars into the Mari tablets, the Tel el-Amarna Letters, the 'inter-testamental' writings, the Dead Sea Scrolls and many other pieces of evidence bearing upon the environment in which the biblical history is set. But this research, entirely justifiable for the purpose of historical understanding, raises in a sharp form the whole question of historical revelation. We began by referring to Scripture as the primary source for our knowledge of God. But if Scripture cannot be fully understood without drawing upon other sources of information, does this mean that these other sources are also 'revealed'? Should we expect to find significant intimations of God's nature in the psalms of the Dead Sea Sect which are not present in the Psalms of David? May there be further 'revealed truth' about God still awaiting the archaeologist's spade?

It may have been in reaction to these paradoxical implications of the historical approach to Scripture that there has recently appeared, in the form of 'Canon Criticism', a new emphasis on the 'givenness' of the biblical material as such. A certain priority must always be given to certain events and certain historical developments by virtue of the fact that they are the subject of Scripture, and must therefore be expected to contribute, one way or another, to our knowledge of God. The importance accorded to extra-biblical sources may vary from time to time: it is in principle impossible to define exactly where sacred history ends and secular history begins. But this again is a significant pointer to the nature of God himself. If we are to be so bold as to say (as Scripture authorises us to do) that God is involved in a particular strand of human history, it would clearly be pushing this way of speaking too far to claim that we always know exactly where God's involvement begins and where it ends.

THE END OF THE STORY

There is one further feature of narrative which is prominent in the Bible and which has caused a good deal of trouble to interpreters. A story, if it is to have power and meaning, needs not only to have shape and consistency; it needs also to have an ending. Indeed in some ways, as some literary critics in recent years have emphasised, the end is the most important part of the story. Stories are ambiguous and enigmatic until we know the ending or denouement, and this is as true of the story that the Bible tells as it is of any other. If we are to take seriously the notion that God is such that his relationship with human beings can be spelt out in narrative form, then the narrative, if it is to convey the truth and meaning, must have an ending. This is true of the Old Testament, where the history of Israel is consistently told in the expectation of the fulfilment of God's promises – or of the severity of his judgement – in the future. It is true also of the New Testament; but here it presents a problem. For now the conviction that the narrative of God's dealings with his people must have an end takes the form of an actual proclamation by Jesus and (for a time, at least) by his followers that the end of the story is not merely inevitable but imminent.

For centuries this disturbing aspect of Jesus's message was quietly ignored or interpreted away. But since Albert Schweitzer brought it once again into the foreground of New Testament study in the early years of this century, scholars have wrestled with the apparent non-fulfilment of Jesus's predictions after two thousand years of continuing history. There is, they have suggested, an inevitable tension in the gospel between an 'already' and a 'not yet'. Jesus brought into the world totally new possibilities for human living in relation to God; the essential conditions for the fulfilment of God's promises are already here. But the realities of judgement and ultimate salvation – the necessary 'ending' of the story – remain in the future; and if these realities are to influence conduct they must be imagined to be about to break upon humanity now, 'in this generation'. Taken as a chronological prediction, Jesus's reading of the future seems to convict him of error. Emptied of any reference to historical prediction, it ceases to exert influence on the thinking and conduct of his followers.

There seems to be no universally accepted escape from this dilemma, though in fairness it should be acknowledged that a number of respected scholars have offered other interpretations of what Jesus expected for his own 'generation'. Some see an anticipation of 'end' judgement in the destruction of Jerusalem by the Romans in AD 70; some argue that Jesus was referring at least in part to the events of the Resurrection and Pentecost. No single solution, however, commands universal assent. It may be better, once again, to accept it as a necessary consequence of the biblical perception that God may be made the subject of a narrative. A story takes place in time, and must have an ending. If God is such that he can be the subject of our story, then he can validly be conceived as working within time towards a final denouement. But to press this way of speaking to the point of asking exactly when the end is to take place is to force God into a human mould. It is clearly not true either that God wills an eternal and unchanging order on earth or that he intended an intervention such as was expected by Jesus's first followers, if not by Jesus himself. A 'doctrine of God' cannot be constructed out of either proposition. The revelation of God in Scripture serves rather to validate the idea of a God who is involved in the temporal flow of history and is the subject of a narrative that must necessarily (if it is to be understood) move towards an ending. But the contradictions which arise from pursuing this way of speaking too far warn us of its limitations, and encourage us continually to sift and enlarge our imagining of the reality to which such language points.

INCONSISTENCIES AND CORRECTIONS

By way of introduction to Scripture as the primary source of the knowledge by which we are to interpret and control our experience of God, we have drawn attention to two particular features of it: its origins in community and its narrative content. These two especially are crucial for understanding the way in which an ancient written testimony may give authentic intimations of the truth about God. Other features could doubtless be added which made the same point – the prominence of poetical forms of expression, for example – but it happens that the two chosen are of particular concern to modern biblical scholarship. They are, moreover, sufficient to illustrate the point that if any written documents can claim to be a revelation of the truth about God, they must presuppose both that God is such that the literary forms used can say something meaningful about him, and also that he must necessarily transcend the models which Scripture offers for understanding him. Like the hypotheses used by scientists to describe the physical universe, the models used in the Bible to describe God are valid up to a certain point of experience and understanding, but (in theory, at least) they are corrigible in the light of new challenges to faith and further moments of revelation. But, as in science, the correction does not necessarily invalidate the existing model. It can continue in use as a guide for thought and conduct, until good reason has been shown for discarding it.

This process of correction of one model by another (which nevertheless allows a certain validity to the corrected model) can be seen both in the study of the Bible and in the Bible itself. Reference was made earlier to the problem created for all interpreters and theologians by the fact that statements can be found in the Bible about God (and about many other things) which appear to contradict one another. For many centuries this caused no difficulty to believers; indeed such instances were taken to indicate that the true meaning was to be found below the surface of the text. By various methods of interpretation (all nowadays customarily but loosely labelled 'allegorical') the subject of the passage and many of its details were taken to stand for other realities, perhaps in the sacred history, perhaps in the life of the Christian. These methods have now been generally discarded as a method of critical study; but once their limitations are recognised, they can still be used – and in fact regularly are used in particular situations – for devotional purposes.

A more 'scientific' strategy for dealing with inconsistencies was the consequence of a Darwinian 'evolutionary' approach being combined with a literary analysis of the Old Testament. According to this, a 'development' can be traced from the 'primitive' ideas of earlier strands to the more 'advanced' ideas of the later. Apparent contradictions can then be accounted for as representing different stages in this development. Subsequent scholarship has found great difficulty with this theory. For one thing, the literary sources of the Old Testament are extremely difficult to date objectively, and the argument can be dangerously circular: a certain conception of God is 'primitive' because it occurs in an early text, but we judge that the text is early only because the conception is primitive. In fact it seems impossible to trace an orderly evolution of religious ideas in the Old Testament; yet the evolutionary approach, once again, retains a certain validity as an explanation of some of the apparent changes and inconsistencies in Old Testament thought, as indeed it does as a tool in the study of all the great religions.

Other strategies have been attempted. For a time, a 'Biblical Theology' seemed possible. Under an over-arching concept, such as 'Covenant' or 'Kingdom', it was hoped that apparently competing ideas about God could be brought into harmony and a single set of theological propositions distilled from the Bible as a whole. This enterprise has in its turn been generally abandoned, and has given place to a recognition that different tendencies and schools coexisted within the one religion of Israel, and were never fully reconciled with one another. These frequent shifts of approach have often caused members of the Church to be sceptical or distrustful of the whole scholarly enterprise. Surely Scripture can be allowed to speak for itself without the help of whatever learned hypothesis happens to be fashionable at the moment? Such scepticism and distrust may sometimes be deserved. Theologians, like all academics, are capable of advancing views and hypotheses so extreme or so implausible that common sense rightly refuses to be led by them. But for the most part the suggested comparison with the necessary corrigibility of scientific hypotheses encourages a more respectful attitude. New hypotheses may improve on the old, but they do not altogether supersede them; and the continuing process testifies to the reality of that which the hypotheses seek to illumine: God himself.

Christians in fact are familiar with this process of self-correction even within the Bible. It is present in a sharp form in the relationship between the Old and New Testaments. Why do Christians still read the Old Testament? To a large extent the 'new covenant' of Jesus Christ is clearly a 'correction' of the old. Yet the Church continues to reverence the Old Testament, not just as an aid to understanding the New (which it is), but as a source of revelation about God. It too is 'the Word of the Lord'. The fact that so much has been corrected by the teaching of Jesus does not invalidate the Old Testament, any more than Einstein has invalidated Newton. It is rather that the perspectives introduced by Jesus (as by Einstein) have immensely widened the field of understanding and made previously accepted ways of 'reading' the universe inadequate.

THE FINALITY OF JESUS

Here, at last, we come to the heart of the matter. In the faith of Christians, Jesus Christ himself represents the most radical 'correction' of ideas about God that the world has ever known. In him there is a finality and authority such that no comparable correction is to be expected again within human history. He does not necessarily invalidate all that is said about God in the Old Testament, or even in other world religions. But by his suffering, death and resurrection he significantly enlarges the range of human experience which can be 'read' as a testimony to the love and the power of God; and in his teaching he offers new 'models' of understanding which go far beyond what was available before. How does Jesus possess this exceptional authority to reveal the nature of God? Some would say that it was the unique event of the Resurrection which confirmed the truth of the revelation he offered; and an influential school of New Testament scholars would argue that this can be documented by historical study. But Jesus's authority depends also on a uniquely intimate relationship between himself and God, such that the models proposed by him for speaking about God have an authority that comes from an exceptional degree of personal knowledge. Does this mean that Christ was God-like, or even (as the Church affirms) God? The question is raised already in the New Testament, and the debate continues to this day. That different views are possible, both about the evidence of the New Testament itself, and about its implications for a Christian doctrine of God and of Christ, is a reminder of the inevitable imperfection and corrigibility of the models which we use for our understanding of God. But the continuance of the enquiry, and the vitality of the faith which sustains it, testifies to the reality of the God with whom we have to do, and to the ultimate authority of Jesus as the prime source of our knowledge and experience of him.

When we come, then, to ask in detail what Scripture says about the nature of God, there will always be a certain provisionality about any answer we can give. The very nature of the Bible's witness to God – its basis in the experience of a community, its emphasis on speaking about him in historical narrative, and so forth – allows us to form certain conclusions about God, and also to expect a certain consistency in the descriptions of his character. But the inadequacy of any language to encompass so great a reality must prevent us from achieving a perfectly systematic account of biblical theology, and warn us that any one account of the biblical evidence is likely to need correction (without thereby becoming obsolete) in the light of new perceptions and methods. What follows in the next two chapters claims to be no more than a survey of present scholarly opinion. drawing together those strands of the biblical witness which are most relevant to our enquiry. As such they describe a part – indeed a very important part – of the total resources available in the search for a doctrine of God. In a few decades' time such an analysis will, no doubt, look very different, just as it looked different a few decades ago. But, if we truly understand the nature of the biblical witness, this ought to strengthen, not shake, our Christian confidence in the reality of the God to whom this testimony points and in the primacy of Scripture as the path to our discovery of him.

5

The God of Jesus

The Christian understanding of God begins from the Scriptures, and this means the whole Bible, not just the New Testament. The Bible is the record of one people's experience of God, which reached a climax of unique importance in the person of Jesus Christ. Christ marks a turning point, because one of the effects of the movement which he began – the Christian Church – was to make the religious heritage of Israel available to all people. At the same time the estrangement of church and synagogue, coinciding with the shattering effect of the Jewish War and the fall of Jerusalem, led to a parting of the ways between Jews and Christians, and to the emergence of Rabbinic Judaism in separation from Christianity. But the religion of the Old Testament is the common property of both Christians and Jews, and the Christian doctrine of God cannot be understood except on this basis.

As argued in the preceding chapter, the Bible is not a treatise about God, but a collection of writings which together convey glimpses of the story of Israel, and of individuals within Israel, in relation to God through many centuries. The books of the Old Testament have themselves had a complex literary history. Almost all of them have been edited and re-edited, or expanded with fresh material, before reaching their final form in the Bible as we know it. Thus the very first chapters of Genesis contain ideas of God which in all probability came from different periods and backgrounds. People in the time of Jesus, however, had little sense of this kind of historical development, so that it is the overall impression of the final form of the text, read in a context of worship, which shaped their understanding of God. Thus the presuppositions about God which were shared by Jesus and the Jews of his time include ideas which can be traced far back into primitive Israelite thought, and also insights gained through later experiences. These belong within a concept of God which underlies not only Judaism and Christianity but also Islam.

The story of Israel can thus be seen as a voyage of discovery. The knowledge of God is acquired gradually through the vicissitudes of many centuries by a nation which regarded itself as God's special people. But this is to look at it from a purely human point of view. It is also possible to see it as a story of the activity of God. Through the history of his people, God has been working out his purpose of creating a people capable of responding to his gracious will, and this is not for the sole benefit of Israel alone, but for all the peoples on earth. It is only when both ways of looking at the Bible's story are given full value that an authentic religious experience results. For religion is the bond between God and humankind. This bond is sometimes referred to in the Bible as the covenant between God and his people.

The Old Testament, which contains this story of God's creation of his people and of that people's growth in knowledge of God, is a collection of those books which were most highly valued as sacred writings by the Jews in the time of Christ. Most of these books were completed by 300 BC, though Daniel and Esther, at least, are most probably later. In addition there are other venerated writings from the last three centuries before Christ which were not in the end received by Judaism into its canon of sacred Scripture, and about which Christians have differed, some including them in the Canon, others, like the Church of England, placing them in the secondary category of Apocrypha. In modern times the extant Jewish religious literature of this period has been enlarged by the discovery of the Dead Sea Scrolls, which have added greatly to our knowledge of the life and thought of

Judaism in the time of Christ. Thus, when we try to assess the understanding of God shared by Jesus and his contemporaries, we need to take into account the information provided by all these writings. To confine attention to the Old Testament alone would be misleading for understanding the rise both of Christianity and of Rabbinic Judaism.

The beginnings of Christianity are documented by the books of the New Testament. In this case the collection of writings is not the fruit of centuries of literary evolution. Nevertheless, behind the Gospels in particular there is still a complex process in which, for example, oral traditions, popular memories of Jesus, missionary preaching and written material have all played their part. Moreover, the Gospels are not modern critical biographies, aiming at impartiality, but the work of writers who were deeply committed to the gospel message. There are areas of literary overlap between Matthew, Mark and Luke, but these reveal some of the ways in which the evangelists felt free to alter or expand or abbreviate their sources. The influence of a doctrinal interest, too, must be allowed for in all four Gospels. The Gospel of John raises particular questions from this point of view, and scholars are divided on the question of its value as historical record, while recognising its great importance as a presentation of the meaning of Jesus for faith.

These factors must be taken into account when we attempt to discover the central teaching of Jesus, and to see how the Church's faith in Jesus affected the Christian concept of God. The books of the New Testament belong to the time when Christian faith was in the process of being hammered out. Thus we shall need to look at the evidence of the New Testament for two different purposes. In the present chapter we shall be concerned with the understanding of God in ancient Israel, in Judaism between the Old and New Testament periods, and in the teaching of Jesus himself, and we shall be especially interested in the features which characterise, and may be held to differentiate, his concept of God. In the next chapter we shall try to see how the Church's faith in Jesus has brought about a distinctively Christian doctrine of God without denying the Old Testament inheritance.

THE GOD OF THE OLD TESTAMENT

The sheer variety of the literature of the Old Testament, and the length of time which went into its making, counsel caution in embarking on a composite description of its witness to Israel's understanding of God. There are, however, certain constants of fundamental importance. Moreover, though it is possible to perceive primitive ideas which are eventually discarded, the process is not a matter of deliberate change, but of a gradual enlarging of perspective, which eventually effects radical correction without denial of the past. The stability of Israel's concept of God is in fact one of the most striking features of Old Testament religion. In what follows, four leading ideas will be taken in order to focus the main themes.

(a) The God of the Old Testament is always and everywhere conceived as a *personal* being. From the ancient stories of the patriarchs in Genesis to the latest retelling of Israel's history in the books of Chronicles, the God whom we meet is one who makes plans and implements them, enjoys successes and experiences frustration when human beings resist his will, changes his mind and formulates revised plans for reaching his ultimate goals. He maintains personal relations with his people through speech. Those who are close to him, like Abraham, may have conversations with him. He addresses the people as a whole through prophets. When a prophet says 'These are the words of Yahweh' he speaks in the manner of a state messenger who says 'These are the words of King So-and-so'; they are uttered by the agent, but they come from the master. Sometimes, it seems, the prophets believed that they heard with their own ears words which God himself made audible; sometimes, perhaps, they saw themselves as putting into their own words convictions felt within, which they believed came from God. The laws of Israel similarly are expressed as words of Yahweh rather than the enactments of a king or a religious teacher.

The actual content of Yahweh's speech also reflects his personhood. He gives vent to the feelings of a person, not only love, joy and compassion, but also regret, jealousy and anger. Though he can be likened to a lion or a rock, most characteristically people think of him in human terms. So we find him compared to a king or a shepherd, to a father, mother, husband or potter. He is the dynamic, living God. The ban on images of God in the Law actually reinforces this. For the lively, energetic, moving, acting and speaking God of Israel can never be captured in a static image.

Being personal involves relationships on both sides. God is not only one who speaks, but also one who is addressed. The Psalms exhibit astonishing freedom in addressing God. Besides expressions of love and gratitude and trust, there are uninhibited grief and rage and doubt. The people of Israel always assumed that God is real enough and personal enough to appreciate the sharing of their hopes and fears; that he has not only ears to hear but feelings to be aroused and energy to be activated. The God of Israel is one who invites his children to the shared speech of conversation, and thus to shared involvement in his world.

(b) For, secondly, the God of the Old Testament is himself involved in the world. At first, perhaps, conceived as a clan God, concerned for his own people, in the classic period of Old Testament religion he is perceived as the sole creator of the world. Though he is in himself independent of the world, and far too great to be in any way confined to it or captured in it, he is its creator and directs its story. He looks after the destiny of his people. It can even be said that he has a covenant with them to be their God, that he has chosen one people out of all the nations as his own. By the sixth century BC the covenant concept has been extended to creation, and the bow in the cloud in the story of the flood

is the sign that Yahweh will never again destroy human-kind. Moreover God's purpose is the ultimate good of his people, and even disasters are intended for their correction. The prophets again and again upbraid the people for their failures to keep the covenant, and threaten dire punishment. But if Israel will only learn the lesson of its disobedience, there is always hope for the future.

God's involvement with the world is not confined to national and international affairs, set in the great sweep of history from first Beginning to final End. He is also the source of the world's stability and life. He provides breath for all living creatures, and rain that the plants may grow. He is involved in human life as provider, healer and friend. Sometimes, as in Proverbs, it is too easily assumed that his providence is certain to issue in prosperity for the righteous and misfortune for the wicked. But as this does not accord with experience, it is not surprising to find Ecclesiastes putting forward a counter-interpretation of life, uncharacteristic of Israel's general understanding of God; and at times deeply cynical and pessimistic. This problem, inherent in all theistic religion, is faced at a deeper level in the agonising of Job and in the prophecy of the Suffering Servant in Isaiah 53.

(c) Thirdly, for all his personal qualities and involvement with the world, Yahweh is not just a human person writ large. The Old Testament's way of referring to his distinctiveness is by speaking of him as the *Holy One.* Holiness denotes the mysterious otherness of God, belonging to the heavenly realm, demanding the response of awed worship on the part of humankind, terrifying his people with thunder and portents when he gives the Law on Mount Sinai. God's holiness is inseparable from his righteousness and love. He is both merciful and just, and both these qualities inspire awe. Isaiah, who in his vision heard the seraphim cry 'Holy, holy, holy' (6.3), asserts that 'The Lord of Hosts is exalted in justice, and the holy God shows himself holy in righteousness' (5.16). Thus the concept of holiness, which is not necessarily an ethical idea

in itself, is in Israel's religious consciousness inseparably bound up with ethical qualities. Those characteristics, mentioned earlier, which make it possible to speak of Yahweh as personal, are not in conflict with his holiness.

The link between God's holiness and his love is captured in a phrase from Isaiah's northern contemporary Hosea, whose perception of Yahweh breaks through the stereotypes of power and authority to the tenderness of God. Hosea's understanding of God's involvement with Israel is expressed in terms of a parent with a wayward child, whose love will not let him go, however far he strays. 'I will not exercise my fierce anger . . . for I am God and not man, the Holy One in your midst' (Hos. 11.9). Such is the steadfast love of Yahweh that, even at the moment of wrath, one can plead with him to remember mercy (Exod. 32.11; Hab. 3.2).

Justice and love also come to be expressed in the Law of Moses, which is the basis of the covenant between Yahweh and his people. In Deuteronomy the Law is presented to the people as the expression of God's love and his gift for their good; and they in their turn must respond with obedience and with love for God. Similarly, in the Priestly strand of the legal codes of the Old Testament the people themselves are to be holy in order to maintain fellowship with the holy God. Rites of purification are provided and sacrifices are prescribed to maintain the holiness of the people.

(d) Fourthly, the love and justice of God are held together as two sides of one coin by the insistence of the Old Testament that God is *one*. Though he may be pictured as holding court surrounded by angels, he is never the centre of a mythology of squabbling and intriguing gods, like the gods of Canaan and Babylon. The attributes and functions of God are not split up among a multiplicity of divinities. The temptation to do this, which recurs over a long period of Israel's religious history, is considered to be apostasy from Yahweh, a choosing to 'go after other gods'. Nor is there anything in the Old Testament to

suggest an ultimate dualism, whereby the principles of love and justice are ascribed to different gods. The Law makes the solemn affirmation 'Yahweh our God, Yahweh one' (Deut. 6.4) and the great anonymous prophet of the sixth century BC has Yahweh say, 'Maker of light and creator of darkness, maker of peace and creator of evil, I Yahweh do all these things' (Isa. 45.7).

Nevertheless we have to beware of oversimplification. From the earliest time the Spirit of Yahweh was spoken of in a way that almost separates it from Yahweh himself. The Spirit comes mightily upon Jephthah (Judges 11.29) and Saul (1 Sam. 10.6) and speaks through the prophets (1 Kings 22.24). But this does not mean that the Spirit is thought of as a separate god. It is a faculty or attribute of God himself, objectified in order to speak of God's power within persons without compromising his essential otherness from humankind. In later times the Wisdom of God (sometimes personified as a woman) is treated in the same way.

Furthermore the Old Testament embraces the idea of angelic spirits, both good and bad, who are subordinate to Yahweh and influence the thoughts and actions of humankind. This idea becomes much more prominent in the later period, particularly in Daniel, the Apocrypha and the Dead Sea Scrolls, probably as a result of Persian influence. One such spirit is the Adversary (the 'Satan'), who is used by God to put people to the test. From the fourth century BC onwards he becomes more prominent as the author of evil, and this shows how the Jews at this later time were reluctant to attribute evil to the direct action of God. Nevertheless God always remains in ultimate control. If the course of human history is interpreted in terms of the conflict between cosmic powers of good and evil, the defeat of evil is certain, because God will triumph in the end.

Finally, if God is in control of human history, it follows that his goodness can be fully displayed only in the salvation of his people. The vicissitudes of Israel's history are always seen in relation to the unfolding of the will of

God. The suffering of the Babylonian exile is his punishment for the nation's sins. At the same time there is always hope of restoration and a glorious future. The Messianic hope began as simply hope for the restoration of the Davidic monarchy after the exile was over. Only when that proved to be impossible did Messianism take more varied forms.

But the oneness of God also led some prophetic souls towards universalism. The one God of all the earth could not be indifferent to the fate of the other nations. This was perceived, for example, by the author of Isaiah 40-55, the anonymous prophet already mentioned, who spoke of Israel's vocation to be 'a light to the nations, that my salvation may reach to the end of the earth' (Isa. 49.6). But such glimpses of universalism are rare in the Old Testament.

BETWEEN THE OLD AND NEW TESTAMENTS

The Old Testament closes with the story unfinished, and the scene is still not set for the entry of Jesus on the stage. The restoration which followed the Exile, late in the sixth century BC, did not fulfil the expectations voiced by the prophets. Israel now became a province in the empire of a foreign overlord. After the conquests of Alexander the Great a popular idealisation of Greek culture threatened the distinctive understandings of other faiths. Local religious practices everywhere were assimilated to the Greek pattern, and the worship of the universal God of Heaven was widely absorbed into the worship of Zeus. Inevitably there were Jews who wished to bring their culture and religion into line with these tendencies, and they had the favour of the imperial power. The Maccabean Revolt of 167 BC was not just a struggle against foreign domination. It was primarily a life and death stand for the traditions of Israel's faith, focused on the right to live and to worship God according to the Law. Thus the biblical understanding of God was central to the issue. Men and women gave their lives on behalf of God's Law. The memory of the

Maccabean martyrs dominates the religion of Judaism in New Testament times. It also explains the tenacity with which the Law was held and promoted in the Jewish communities throughout the Greco-Roman world.

The success of the revolt, however, did not produce the fulfilment of Israel's ideals. The new rulers, successors to the Maccabees, held on to their precarious independence by wars and diplomacy among the superpowers, and themselves became corrupted in the process. It was the period of the emergence of sects and parties. An open attitude towards the faith of others was maintained by the Sadducees, who combined religious conservatism with a lofty philosophical outlook. Drawn chiefly from the aristocratic and high-priestly families, their first concern was for the safety of the state. The spirit which animated the revolt lived on in the Pharisees, the Essenes and the Zealots. The Pharisees were concerned to promote the religion of the people, and encouraged exact keeping of the Law to this end. The Dead Sea Scrolls have revealed a sect (probably the Essenes) which had opted for complete separation from temple and state, which were regarded by them as hopelessly corrupt. The sect was devoted to study of the Law, and regarded itself as the sole heir to the destiny of Israel in the plan of God. 'Zealots' is a term loosely employed to cover all those who looked to a holy war of the Maccabean type to bring about the salvation of Israel. To others, however, the times were too troubled for them to discern any divine plan of salvation. Nevertheless despair leads to hope against hope, and many believed that the intervention of God would not be long delayed.

The Judaism into which Jesus was born was thus different from the world of the Old Testament. Brought up in this setting, his understanding of God and his teaching about God naturally take some of their colour from the characteristic emphases of Judaism in his time, as these had been formed in response to the pressure and experiences of the Maccabean age. Four features in particular need to be borne in mind.

(a)   First, the centrality of the Law in Jewish religion had been greatly enhanced by the struggle. At a time when God's power and otherness were dramatically magnified by the experience of life in the enlarged perspectives of the Greco-Roman world, there was a danger that his greatness and purity might place him altogether beyond the reach of human littleness and sinfulness. But because the transcendent God was imminent in the Law, love for God could be expressed in love for the Law, and attention to its detailed demands could ensure that a person was in right relationship with God. The Law was not only central to worship, but touched people at every point in their daily lives. The natural description of devout people was that they walked according to the Law blamelessly (cf. Luke 1.6). Conversely less devout Jews tended to care less about the niceties of the Law, especially on matters that appeared irksome and pointless.

(b)   Secondly, the troubled times leading to the Maccabean Revolt had led many devout people to seek for visionary experiences which would reveal God's will for his people, and so bring reassurance. They hoped to penetrate the secrets of Heaven and to determine the divine plan for the future. The apocalyptic literature comes from this circle, Daniel 7-12 and Revelation (a Christian work) being the best known examples. It is important to realise that real and profound religious experiences lay behind the production of this kind of literature, which continued throughout the New Testament period. Such experiences implied a direct knowledge of God and his will, comparable to the inspiration of the Old Testament prophets. This carried with it the danger of conflict with those who held that the Law was the sole repository of the revealed knowledge of God (cf. Ecclesiasticus 34.1-8).

(c)   A third feature of the times is the expectation of a Messiah. It has already been observed that many were convinced that God would soon intervene in history to establish his own rule everlastingly. Disenchantment with

the successors to the Maccabees led many to long for the restoration of the house of David, a king who would bring freedom and justice to the land. This was only one of the forms which the Messianic hope took in this period, but all were agreed that the era of justice and freedom would come only by the act of God in fulfilment of his age-long promises. But how would that act be mediated? Would it be by the political activism of the Zealots, who saw themselves as under solemn obligation to free the land from foreign rule, and eventually precipitated the Jewish War of AD 66–70? Or were the devout called not to act themselves, but only to 'look for the consolation of Israel' (Luke 2.25)? The Pharisees, who were opposed to political activism but shared the hope of the Messiah, encouraged patient waiting for God to intervene in his own good time. The visionary literature in general saw God's action in cosmic rather than political terms, though it implied that this action would not be long delayed. It sometimes portrayed a specific programme of events: cosmic disturbances terminating the present world order, the resurrection of the dead, the judgement of the nations, and the fulfilment of God's purpose of endless blessing for the righteous.

(d) This notion of the resurrection of the dead constituted a fourth point of importance in the faith of Judaism in the time of Jesus. In the Old Testament the state of the dead is virtually non-existence, cut off from the joy of the presence of Yahweh. By New Testament times, however, most Jews had come to believe in a future state in which the injustices of earthly life are done away. Here again the Maccabean experience had been crucial. Between the individual's death and the general resurrection the soul, separated from the body, would go to a place of waiting, where the reversal of destiny for the successful oppressor and the undeserving sufferer could already begin. Especially in the teaching of the Pharisees, rewards and punishments after death became the sanctions of moral teaching. God was seen as the judge who weighs the life of the

individual to see how far he has met the demands of the Law. Thus Judaism affirms that God's sovereignty extends to the dead as well as to the living, so that the righteous of every generation are destined to have their share in the everlasting kingdom.

JESUS AND GOD

For reasons that have already been explained it is not easy to make a synthesis of the teaching of Jesus out of the Gospels. But certain points stand out which command agreement even among the most cautious scholars.

We can begin from the first of the four features just mentioned, the place accorded to the Law in contemporary Jewish spirituality. The transcendent God was thought of as immanent in the Law, and this meant a shift of the emotional centre to the Law itself. A similar tendency can also be seen in the exaggerated use of reverential language, whereby mention of God was avoided or alternatively expanded with epithets of majesty. It is well known that by this time the name of God was never normally spoken, even when reading the scriptures.

But the most notable feature of Jesus's spirituality was that, without in any way denying the Law, he did not relate to God through the Law but directly as 'Father', and invited his hearers to share in the same relationship. Though God was indeed known and addressed as 'Father' in Judaism, the image was not a prevalent one, and as far as we know the Aramaic word 'Abba' was not used to address God in prayer in contemporary Judaism. It was the family word, implying both affection and respect, used not only by children, but also by the disciples of a rabbi. It thus suggests an attitude of humility, obedience and reverence, as well as one of dependence, security and confidence.

There is thus a new richness of content in Jesus's concept of God. Fatherly attributes come to the fore in his teaching. God is one who loves, cares, gives, listens, welcomes, seeks, accepts, forgives, provides. The concept is positive, and there is little hint of the darker father-image associated with the idea of the angry God. The fatherly love of God extends also to expectations and demands. It is particularly striking that in his anguished prayer in Gethsemane Jesus prays, 'Abba, Father, all things are possible for you. Take this cup from me. Yet not what I want but what you want' (Mark 14.36). God is the Father who loves him, and therefore Jesus can bring to him his longing for relief. God is also the Father who has expectations of him and therefore Jesus accepts that ultimately his will is what counts.

Whatever the sense in which Jesus saw his own sonship as special, he emphasised that God behaves like a father to all, and all are invited to relate to him as his children. He encourages his disciples to pray 'Father . . .', as he himself does. The Lord's Prayer parallels the Gethsemane prayer in working out the implications of God's fatherhood in terms of both authority and caring. For the disciples too, praying to the Father involves the desire for his name to be hallowed and his reign to come, before they can expect him to concern himself with their basic needs for food, forgiveness and protection from evil. He is, as Matthew emphasises, a heavenly Father, one who commands all heaven's resources for the fulfilling of his people's needs, but also one who must be reverenced as the Lord of heaven.

Jesus's conflict with the Pharisees arose from this teaching, because he sought to promote a more direct approach to God, to which the minutiae of the Law were a hindrance rather than a help. The Pharisees, like Jesus himself, were genuinely concerned to raise the standard of religion among the people, but their methods were diametrically opposed to his, because they sought to achieve this aim by stressing exact observance of the details of the Law. But the intensity of the conflict is to be explained by the second of our four points, namely that Jesus belonged with the visionaries of his time and claimed direct authority for his teaching from God. It is clear that he was popularly regarded as a prophet. Not being an ordained rabbi, he had no teaching authority other than his personal claim to divine inspiration. So the conflict concerned not only the substance of his teaching but also his personal authority as a teacher.

The God whom Jesus proclaimed was a God whose intervention in history was imminent: 'The time is fulfilled, and the kingdom of God is at hand; repent and believe in the gospel' (Mark 1.15). This corresponds with the third feature of the intertestamental period. Jesus's teaching, as we should expect, had more in common with the apocalyptic notion of direct action by God than with the political expectation of the Davidic Messiah. In accordance with the Jewish tendency to avoid expressions suggesting that God might be visible, Jesus spoke of the coming of the kingdom of God as a circumlocution for the coming of God himself. And this is the gospel – the good news – because the God who is coming is the God who is already known as Father, and his kingdom will mean blessing for the poor and the sad and the outcast. They will be rich and be glad and have a great reward (Luke 6.20-23).

Jesus preached with a great sense of urgency, because he believed that the time was short (Mark 9.1). But the content of his message referred to the present as well as the future, because his own words, with their impact on his hearers, made God present already through their concentration on the God who was coming. Even as he speaks the reign of God dawns. Already in Jesus's ministry the blind receive their sight, the lame walk, and the poor have the good news preached to them (Matt. 11.4-5).

The implementation of God's kingship turns upside down the expectations of the world and conventional religious tradition. The blessings of God's reign are given, not earned, so that they come to all, no matter how long they have worked for them. The prodigal son finds an unexpected welcome from a prodigally loving father. The child is the model for the receptivity that embraces God's reign, and God's heart fills with joy when one sinner repents (Matt. 20.1-16; Mark 10.15; Luke 15.11-32, 18.9-14).

There is thus no suggestion that there is no need of repentance. Jesus announces an imminent confrontation with God in all his holiness, purity, goodness, mercy and love. It is not enough to point to one's religious status or religious observances, for God's demands extend far beyond the outward righteousness for which these commonly stand. Where the law prohibits murder and adultery, Jesus on behalf of God forbids hatred and lust within the heart. We cannot expect God's forgiveness at the judgement, if we are not willing to forgive others ourselves. And just as the coming day of salvation was already dawning in the ministry of Jesus, so the response to his message from God already anticipates the judgement (Matt. 12.32). To reject his message is to repudiate the Spirit of God himself (12.31).

Jesus is aware that his teaching makes great demands. The reign of God is like a pearl of immense value, which a merchant might sacrifice all his assets to obtain (Matt. 13.46). For the disciple who wants the life of the coming age it is not enough to keep the commandments; he must sell all and give to the poor (Mark 10.21). Response to God's love allows no compromise. The opposition to Jesus will inevitably be reflected in persecution of the disciples. They too must take up their cross and be ready to lose their life in order to save it (Mark 8.34–36).

Jesus did indeed pay with his own life for his fidelity to his mission from God. He was crucified as the Messiah, the king of the Jews, and this implies that, however much he distanced himself from popular political expectations of the Messiah, he saw his role as in some sense having a Messianic character. If the coming day of salvation is already partly fulfilled in his ministry, and if the judgement is anticipated in his words, then he is the agent of God's kingdom which is imminently expected. It is important to realise that his sense of urgency was simply the catalyst of his message from God. The failure of the expectation of the coming of God does not render it invalid. As we shall see in the next chapter, the Church after the resurrection soon began to realise that the mission of Jesus, culminating in his death, was part of the final intervention of God, so that never again could it be claimed that God's decisive act on behalf of the world lay wholly in the future, without regard to what God had already done in Jesus.

Jesus taught that from those to whom much is given, much is expected, and the cross is the ultimate test of his commitment to that message. At the outset of his ministry, it appears, he was tempted to put God's fatherly love to the proof (Matt. 4.1-11). Before his arrest at Gethsemane he was tempted again to seek a way out of the ordeal. But this human shrinking must be set against both his repeated conviction that the danger to his life could not be avoided and his determination to make of his life a sacrifice to God. 'For the Son of man also came not to be served but to serve, and to give his life as a ransom for many' (Mark 10.45). By making of his death a sacrifice, Jesus affirmed his teaching about God, whose power extends beyond the grave (our fourth feature of the intertestamental period), who 'sends rain on the just and on the unjust alike' (Matt. 5.45), and whose will for the salvation of humankind cannot ultimately be thwarted (Luke 12.32). The cross is not something external to Jesus's mission and message, an end imposed upon them by others, but the heart and crown of his life and teaching.

CONCLUSION

The God of Jesus is the God of the Old Testament, personally involved in his creation, holy and one. In him justice and love are held together. His ultimate triumph over evil is sure. Through his Spirit he is the author of all zeal for goodness in humankind. His ears are open to the prayers of his servants, who can speak to him in their hearts.

Jesus must have appeared to his contemporaries as a visionary, a charismatic prophet concerned with the re-newal of religion at a time of great perplexity. Working under a great sense of urgency, he declared that the triumph of God's love was imminent, and that this would be primarily a time of blessing for the oppressed. Renewal is a matter of the heart and the springs of action. It requires a vital relationship with God, whom Jesus teaches his followers to address as 'Father'. Suffering is the test of this relationship, but it cannot destroy the assurance of the ultimate providence of God.

The message of Jesus was addressed to his fellow Jews, and he never questions the validity of the Law. But it is evident that his teaching operates at a deeper level than observance of the Law, and is easily translated into other situations. Thus, though examples are rare in the teaching of Jesus, there are times when he is shown as looking beyond Israel (cf. Matt. 8.10-12). Through Jesus the way is opened for the religious inheritance of Israel to be made available to every people, and the God of Israel can be known as the God and Father of Jesus Christ, Lord and brother of every human being.

6

The God of the Disciples

The history of earliest Christianity shows a very remarkable development in the understanding of God, which eventually found expression in the doctrine of the Trinity, Father, Son and Holy Spirit, three Persons in one God. This formulation was not reached until after New Testament times. But it depends upon the evidence of the New Testament, and so has its origin and justification in the experiences of the first two generations of Christians whose thoughts are reflected in those writings. This chapter will try to enter into the minds of these early followers of Jesus, in order to see how the Christian understanding of God developed in the ways that it did. It will be necessary to pay particular attention to the ways in which they thought of the relationship between Jesus and God, because it is their account of this relationship which is the essential basis of the Trinitarian doctrine.

The aim of the last chapter was to pierce through the work of the evangelists to Jesus himself, to recover, as far as may be, Jesus' own understanding of God. This required a critical handling of the Gospels, whose writers shared a well-developed Christian belief. Scholarly critical procedures are still necessary in any attempt to assess the witness of the New Testament to the earliest expressions of that Christian faith and to its subsequent development within the New Testament period. As before, it will be impossible to do more than provide a tentative reconstruction which takes account of the present state of scholarship.

The starting point must be the common ground in the understanding of God which the disciples, particularly Peter and the other apostles, shared with Jesus himself.

They had grown up with the same Jewish inheritance, and were drawn to him because he spoke to their condition in those perplexing times. They shared the contemporary longing for divine intervention. His teaching had given them grounds for hope, and they had committed themselves whole-heartedly to his mission. Jesus's teaching about God, and his use of the simple address 'Father' in prayer (attested by Paul in Gal. 4.6 and Rom. 8.15, which show that even among Greek-speaking converts the Aramaic form 'Abba' was used) had profoundly affected their convictions as to who Jesus was. They saw him as uniquely the agent and spokesman of God's kingdom, as traditions such as that of Peter's confession at Caesarea Philippi (Mark 8.29), declaring him the Messiah, make plain. In retrospect, too, their beliefs about Jesus were deeply affected by the events leading up to the crucifixion, and especially by his attitude to his own death. Recalling that Jesus had proclaimed the forgiveness of sins in his message of the grace of God's kingdom, they now came to see his laying down of his life as securing that forgiveness.

Any hope that Jesus was the Messiah might have seemed to be irrevocably shattered by his death. The Easter proclamation proves that this was not so. The resurrection of Jesus was immediately cited as the grounds for asserting that Jesus was the Lord's Christ. This vindicated the claim of Jesus to be the spokesman and agent of God's kingdom. As the last chapter showed, the message of Jesus could not be separated from his personal relationship with God. If his disciples were to renew his mission after his death, this would depend on the vindication of his status as one chosen, sent or empowered as God's representative. Hence the first step in the process by which Jesus was given a unique place in relation to God was inextricably bound up with the events which led to the renewal of his Gospel message.

JESUS THE CHRIST

The oldest record of the resurrection of Jesus is the tradition, evidently derived from the Jerusalem church, which Paul quotes in 1 Cor. 15.1–11. This includes what may be regarded as the official list of appearances of the risen Christ, beginning with Peter. Paul adds his own conversion experience on the Damascus road to round off the list. The importance of this passage for our present purpose is that it is not the work of Paul himself, but an authoritative formulation which he is at pains to quote carefully and accurately. It thus provides the oldest evidence we possess for the preaching of the first Christian church.

The statement begins by asserting that 'Christ died for our sins in accordance with the Scriptures' (verse 3). Not only does this take for granted that the death of Jesus was a sacrifice for sins, it also retains the title 'Christ', which means that his death, so far from disproving his Messiahship, is actually seen to be a Messianic act and to accord with the plan of God revealed in scripture. (It is very likely that the Old Testament background chiefly in mind here is the Suffering Servant poem of Isaiah 53.)

Secondly, the tradition affirms of Jesus 'that he was buried, and that he was raised on the third day in accordance with the Scriptures' (verse 4). (This may be a reference to Hos. 5.2, taken as speaking metaphorically of resurrection after three days, but this is not certain.) This ancient summary of faith thus includes in God's plan not only the suffering of the Messiah but also his resurrection. The carefully listed appearances attest his present position as the Messiah in heaven. He is risen, and therefore he is the 'first fruits' (1 Cor. 15.23) of the general resurrection. Unlike the rest of humankind who, as we saw, were believed by many in Judaism to go after death to a place of waiting until the general resurrection and the judgement, Jesus has been raised by God to the throne of honour at his right hand. That this has happened precisely because he is the Messiah is a belief supported from the earliest times by reference to Ps. 110.1, 'The Lord said to my lord, Sit at my right hand, until I make your enemies your footstool', which is quoted or alluded to a number of times in the New Testament. It follows that Jesus still has his Messianic task to perform, and that is to be God's 'right hand man' in the coming divine intervention, when death, the 'last enemy' (1 Cor. 15.26), is destroyed at the general resurrection, and God's plan for humanity is accomplished.

Thus, in renewing the gospel of Jesus, the apostles can assert that the loving forgiveness of God has already been demonstrated in the death of Jesus, and the promised blessings of the kingdom are assured because Jesus's own resurrection indicates that he is already waiting at God's right hand to confer them at the general resurrection and the judgement. The concept of Jesus's Messiahship has been filled out with an original and creative use of scriptural texts to interpret the events of Good Friday and Easter. The present position of Jesus as Messiah and Lord is thus reinforced, and becomes the guarantee of the certainty of the message which Jesus gave, and which is now passed on by his disciples. At the same time, though this moves the person of Jesus to the centre of the proclamation, it in no way reduces Jesus's concept of God. The fact that the early Christians arrived at this fresh understanding of Jesus, and saw him not only as a triumphant but also as a suffering Messiah, makes it absolutely plain that the initiative rests with God, whose love for his human children extends even to involvement in suffering. In the unforgettable words of John 3.16, 'God so loved the world, that he gave his only Son, so that every one who believes in him should not perish but should have eternal life.'

Two more things need to be said before moving on to further developments. First, it is a mistake to suppose that the earliest Christians were puzzled about the identity of Jesus, and by dint of casting in their minds around various options eventually came up with the idea that he must be the Son of God. In the light of the resurrection they had no doubt that Jesus was the Messiah; and it is this affirmation which underlies the central New Testament confession, 'Jesus is Lord'. The various developments in Christology were the result of drawing out the theological implications of this basic confession.

Secondly, the role assigned to the risen Christ as God's agent at the judgement presupposes that this divine intervention was eagerly awaited, as is clear, for example in 1 Thess. 1.9-10. The disciples had this expectation, because they were already hoping for such an action of God when they came to Jesus, and this was the context in which they listened to his preaching. Though much of Jesus's teaching is timeless, it is not convincing to eliminate this expectation altogether from that teaching. Were the disciples, and presumably Jesus himself, simply wrong about this? There is no easy answer to this question; but it can be said without hesitation that both the teaching of Jesus and the proclamation of the disciples contain features which could, and in the long run did, provide a way through. For Jesus the expectation of the coming of God in person, already preached by John the Baptist, was the catalyst of his own teaching on the encounter with the kingdom of God. The coming of this kingdom was, as we have seen, to some extent already present in his own ministry, so that he could perceive authentic signs of the kingdom in the response to his message. For the disciples the sacrificial death of Jesus and his exaltation to the right hand of God were the first stage in the actual intervention of God, so that life under the lordship of Christ again anticipated the future kingdom; and this remains true, however long the final act of the coming of Christ is delayed. The Easter proclamation binds together past, present and future. This is splendidly expressed in Paul's statement concerning the meaning of the eucharist in 1 Cor. 11.26: 'For as often as you eat this bread and drink this cup, you proclaim the Lord's death until he comes.'

JESUS THE SON OF GOD

The idea of Jesus as the exalted Messiah at the right hand of God does not necessarily introduce a change or development into the understanding of God himself. Jesus's understanding of God is taken over by the disciples. His sacrificial death, being seen as God's act of reconciliation with humanity, does of course enlarge their understanding of God's involvement in the suffering of his children. But there is no crossing of the boundary between the man Jesus and God. This might, however, seem to have happened when the title 'Son of God' is used. Several points have to be taken into consideration.

(a)   'Son of God' can have a variety of senses. We are all 'children of God' inasmuch as we are part of his creation, and he is our Father in heaven, as Jesus himself taught. We are specially his children when we do what is pleasing to him (Matt. 5.45). Jesus himself is obviously a son of God in this sense.

(b)   More specialised usages can be seen in such passages as Job 38.7, describing the creation, 'when the morning stars sang together, and all the sons of God shouted for joy'. Here it is the angels who are referred to as 'sons of God'. This possibility is faced and rejected with regard to Jesus in Hebrews 1, where Jesus as *the* Son of God is explicitly differentiated from the angels.

(c)   The phrase can also be used for the Messiah, as in Ps. 2.7, which may be the passage referred to by Paul in Rom. 1.4. Jesus, who is in any case 'descended from David according to the flesh' (verse 3), has by his resurrection been designated Son of God in power. The phrase denotes his status in relation to God, and there is no sense of divine begetting involved. But Jesus the Messiah in his heavenly and exalted state, exalted indeed above the ranks of the angels, clearly has a unique position very close to God. Indeed, the New Testament church's use of Ps. 110.1 ('Sit at my right hand') suggests at the very least a share in God's government of the universe. This is certainly picture language, but picture language has to be used when speaking of the invisible things of heaven.

(d)   This sense of the closeness of Jesus to God was enhanced further by his own spirituality, with its characteristic feature of the address to God as 'Abba'. From the beginning this made a profound impression on the disciples, and it soon led them to assume a special relationship between Jesus and God. From this point of view 'son of God' denotes not only status (the exalted Messiah) but also a relationship to God as Father in something more than the sense in which all of us can be children of God. Jesus is the Son of the Father in an exclusive sense. Paul shows the distinction in Rom.8 by describing Christians as 'adopted' children. The Father and Son relationship is expressed in words attributed to Jesus in Matt. 11.27, and is also an omnipresent theme in the Gospel of John. For John the relationship implied by the 'Abba' form of address has become reciprocal. 'The Father loves the Son' (John 5.20), and Jesus can even say, 'I and the Father are one' (10.30). Jesus in John's Gospel can often appear to be a forbidding figure, but not in his relationship with God, which shows a striking tenderness. Moreover, the disciples themselves can enter into this loving relationship through their relationship with Jesus (14.23). The disciples' experience of union with the risen Christ takes them into the unity which exists between him and the Father (17.20-21). Thus, as Paul saw, Jesus is the focal point for all people of the experience of being a child of God, for all, that is, who can pray to God as 'Abba', in the spirit of Jesus himself.

(e) The sonship of Jesus is thus a matter of relationship. John's word *monogenés* (John 1.18) was wrongly taken in the history of doctrine to denote 'only-begotten' (so AV), but actually means 'unique' (RSV only). It does not carry with it the notion of a divine begetting, nor does it necessarily imply pre-existence. For this idea we must turn to other aspects of the New Testament's witness to the disciples' understanding of Jesus and God.

JESUS THE WORD AND WISDOM OF GOD

The proclamation that Jesus is the Christ opened up a new depth of understanding of personal relationship with God, which is focused in Jesus, but is available to all. The proclamation has, however, other consequences also, because the claim that Jesus is the Messiah is not a timeless statement, but relates to god's purpose and plan. If the general resurrection has been anticipated in Jesus, it means that part of God's plan has been accomplished in him by anticipation. The thought that God has a plan of redemption belongs to the determinism which is characteristic of Judaism in New Testament times. The visionaries of the intertestamental period sought to discover God's plan for the future in the certainty that it was already available in the secrets of heaven, if only these could be unlocked. As we have seen, the disciples interpreted the death and resurrection of Jesus in the light of the Scriptures, in which the events of redemption were revealed in advance, and had now come to pass in his person.

This sense of the divine plan can be seen in Paul's statement that 'When the time had fully come, God sent forth his Son' (Gal. 4.4). This implies that the proper time according to God's plan has been reached. It does not yet amount to a statement of the pre-existence of Jesus himself.

However, when Paul describes Jesus in 1 Cor 1.24 as the true 'Wisdom' of God, his representative through whom alone righteousness, sanctification and redemption from sin are possible (1.30), the discussion is taken further. The equation between Jesus and 'Wisdom' is not developed in this passage. Yet here we have the beginnings of a new understanding of Jesus's person, in which he is regarded as the present expression of a divine Wisdom which existed before time began. Behind this language there is the figure of Wisdom in the Old Testament and intertestamental period, an attribute of God which is personified almost as something separate from him, in much the same way as happens with the Spirit of the Lord. Notable passages for the personification of Wisdom are Proverbs 8, Wisdom of Solomon 6–10 and Ecclesiasticus 24. The same background explains Paul's description of Jesus in 1 Cor. 8.6 as the Lord 'through whom are all things and through whom we exist'. For in these passages Wisdom shares in God's creation and dwells protectively among his people.

Similar ideas occur in Col. 1.15–20, where Jesus is called the 'image' of God who 'exists before everything' (verses 15 and 17). As in the Corinthians passages, Jesus becomes the one who reflects God's nature on earth, having participated before time in his creative activity (verse 16). But in two respects new ground is broken in this passage; and in both cases the writer emphasises the intimate relationship which exists between the Father and the Son. First, the statement in verse 19 that 'in him (the Son) the complete being of God came to dwell' implies that the final self-disclosure which takes place in Jesus, the Messiah, connects once and for all the spheres of natural and revealed religion. Here are the real beginnings of what was later to flower as 'incarnational theology'. Secondly, Jesus is identified as the goal, and not merely the origin, of creation: 'the whole universe has been created through him and for him' (verse 16). Clearly the understanding of God which allows such a place for his creative and recreative agent, who, having shed his blood to reconcile the universe to himself, can now be regarded as 'in all things supreme' (verse 18), marks a step forward of momentous significance.

Outside the Pauline writings a very similar idea is expressed in terms of 'Word' rather than 'Wisdom', using a term which would be familiar to Greeks (from the Stoic philosophers, for example) as well as Jews (e.g. Genesis 1, 'God said . . .'; cf. Ps. 33.6, Wisd. 18.15). The key passages are Heb. 1.1–4 and John 1.1–18. Both echo ideas about Jesus already noted in Corinthians and Colossians. Hebrews 1 declares that the God who 'spoke' in creation and in history through the prophets has now finally and fully spoken to us in his Son for the purposes of a new creation. These verses draw on the poem on Wisdom in the Wisdom of Solomon (7.2–8.1).

In the prologue of John, however, the Word is personified in the manner of the Old Testament Wisdom poems, especially Ecclesiasticus 24. John's choice of 'Word' rather than 'Wisdom' may be due to the need to avoid the personification of Wisdom as a woman, which is found in this and other poetic models ('Wisdom' is a feminine word in both Hebrew and Greek.) For here the Word is not only God's partner in the creation and the light that illumines every human being, but is incarnate in Jesus himself. In him the Word becomes flesh (John 1.14). Thus he is not merely, like the prophets, a person through whom God speaks, but the actual embodiment of the Word of God. Just as the Law, so dear to the Jewish people, was held to be the embodiment of the pre-existent Wisdom (Ecclus. 24.23), so Jesus is the incarnation of the pre-existent Word. Just as the Law, like the manna in the wilderness, was held to be the nourishment of the soul, so Jesus is the true bread from heaven which gives life to the world (John 6.32-33). Just as Hebrews describes him as the 'radiance of God's glory' (Heb. 1.3), so John tells how 'we saw his glory, glory as of a father's only son' (John 1.14). Jesus is the human face of God, and to see him is to see the Father (14.9). He is the incarnate Son; and just as the Wisdom of God at the creation 'was at his side each day, his darling and delight' (Prov. 8.30 NEB), so the Word of God can be called his Son from the beginning. The mutual relation of Father and Son, which is central to the spirituality of Jesus, and which characterises his relationship to God as the exalted Messiah, applies too to the Word of God, of which Jesus is the incarnation. Thus the prayer of Jesus in John 17 includes the thought of the 'glory which I had with thee before the world was made' (verse 5).

It should now be clear that the New Testament precludes the impression that Jesus is a man raised to divinity alongside God to form a second God. It is not, then, a case of the deification of a human being. As the exalted Messiah he is 'the first-born among many brethren' (Rom. 8.29), bringing all humankind into union with God; but as the incarnation of the Word of God he partakes of the nature of God himself, making God accessible to our race in his human life. It is the preaching, healing, loving, suffering Jesus who, as the Word made flesh, has made God known (John 1.18).

The God of the Disciples

THE GOD WHO IS MADE KNOWN

The passages discussed all claim, in their own way, that with the coming of Jesus Christ the Creator is made specially accessible to his creatures. But they also reflect a new and developing appreciation of the *kind* of God who has come in the Son. For example, John's portrait of Jesus as the enfleshed Word of God, who came from the Father (John 10.30, 16.28) and lived among us (1.14), represents a profound understanding of incarnation, and one which was to have a far-reaching effect on subsequent Christian doctrine. But it also contains implications for the Christian view of God himself, whose sovereign purpose 'that the world might be saved' (3.17) was brought about, John shows us, by means of a total self-giving love. The exact quality of that love was manifested in his only Son, crucified and glorified (3.13-17).

The significance which the New Testament gives to the death and resurrection of Jesus offers us a further important insight into the early Christian understanding of God. For in the crucifixion and exaltation of Jesus God enters into human suffering, and is intimately related to his people. He is revealed not only as the providential Father of humankind, who was specially present and active in the life of Christ, but also as the Father of a crucified Son. God's involvement in the ministry and message of Jesus, which constitutes the divine initiative in salvation, extends to his death and resurrection as well.

The passion of Jesus appears from the perspective of history to be utter tragedy. But seen from the divine viewpoint it is the climax of Jesus's declaration of God's love. The sacrificial value of the death of Jesus as an atonement for sin is already declared in the earliest preaching of the disciples (1 Cor. 15.3). The same idea is taken up and expounded in other parts of the New Testament. Thus the writer of 1 Peter holds up before his readers, as an example for them to follow, the way in which on our behalf Jesus shared, but also transformed, the tragedy of human suffering (1 Pet. 2.20-25).

97

Among the New Testament witnesses Paul and John, in particular, highlight the significance of the cross for the understanding of God. Paul indicates, first of all, that God entered into the suffering which Christ's passion involved. 'He who did not spare his own Son', he says, 'but delivered him up on behalf of us all, how shall he not also with him freely give us all things?' (Rom. 8.32). Here the fact that it is the Father who has delivered up his Son preserves the divine initiative, so that the human tragedy can be seen to have its providential side. But because it is God himself who 'does not spare' Jesus, in that gift to us he is deeply involved in the total act of redemptive suffering.

The same thought is reflected in John, who goes further than Paul in his delineation of the nature of God's gift by stressing the filial obedience of Jesus to the Father, and by relating that to the cross as its culminating point. Jesus, according to John, accepted death as the fullest expression of his sonship. The proof that he is 'from above' is seen in the fact that 'the Son of man *must* be lifted up' in death (John 3.14). But the cross itself provides the ultimate demonstration of the moral unity between Jesus and the Father (cf. John 8.28), and in this way not only reveals the obedience of the Son in completing the work which the Father gave him to do (17.4), but also characterises the nature of the God who initiated the work of salvation in the first place. By 'giving' his Son to the world which he loved, the Father, in John's view, entered fully into the suffering which that entailed.

John's account of the death of Jesus as 'glorification' brings out another insight in the early Christian understanding of God. For the death and resurrection of Jesus not only made the first believers aware of God's involvement in his suffering world, they also spoke of the new and permanent relationship with the Father which is possible through the Son. When John describes the approaching death of Jesus, or his actual crucifixion, as a 'glorification' (e.g. John 7.39, 12.23), this implies that in the very moment of 'lifting up' in agony it is possible to see the exaltation of Jesus to his designated place 'at the right hand of God' (Heb. 10.12, cf. Ps. 110.1), with its promise of final blessedness for all who believe. Similarly, what began in the incarnation was completed by the cross. Just as during the earthly ministry of Jesus the life-giving presence of God was brought to humankind, so in a final act of self-giving on the cross, through which Jesus returns to the Father (John 13.3), the eternal life or 'glory' of God becomes available to every believer for all time.

The spiritual implications of such a 'glorification' are very rich indeed. Because the Word of God has dwelt among us (John 1.14), it is possible not only to see God but also to abide in him through Christ (17.21). Such an intimate indwelling, furthermore, is complemented by the fact that God abides in the believers through the risen Jesus (14.23). Paul uses different language to make the same vital point. The life and death and resurrection of Jesus together are the basis for a mutual indwelling: God in us (1 Cor. 6.20) and we in God (Col. 3.3). The church has peace with God through Jesus Christ (Rom. 5.1); and its spiritual inheritance is such that its members can be described as 'God's heirs and Christ's fellow-heirs' (8.17). The vision is completed by the author of Revelation, who glimpses a 'new heaven and a new earth' in which God dwells at last among his people. 'He will dwell among them and they shall be his people, and God himself will be with them' (Rev. 21.1-3).

THE HOLY SPIRIT

How is this new quality of divine life, to which the New Testament in varying ways bears witness, to be sustained on earth? The answer to that question takes up the Old Testament teaching on the spirit of Yahweh, generally referred to in New Testament times as the Holy Spirit. From the first Jesus claimed that his prophetic ministry was inspired by the Holy Spirit (Matt. 12.28), and indeed his baptism by John was interpreted as his Messianic anointing by the Spirit (Mark 1.10-11). According to prophecy the coming age would be marked with a general outpouring of the spirit (Joel 2.28, cf. Acts 2.17), and this could already be seen in the charismatic gifts in the church (1 Corinthians 12).

In the writings of Paul, however, there is an explicitly Christian development in the understanding of the Holy Spirit. In Paul's thought the Spirit indwells both the church and the believer; and the meeting-place of the spirit of God and our spirit is the believing community, and that community alone (cf. 1 Cor. 3.16-17, 6.19). Moreover the Spirit's help is a necessary precondition of Christian faith (1 Cor. 12.3). From such starting points arises Paul's further insight that only when the Spirit indwells the church can its continuing life be sustained, and the gifts of God regularly manifested (12.4-10).

John develops in a highly significant manner the understanding of the Spirit noted elsewhere in the New Testament. To some extent John shares with the other Gospel writers an 'endowment' view of the Spirit. In his account of Christ's baptism too the Spirit descends on Jesus 'as a dove from heaven' (John 1.32*a*), and after the resurrection Jesus is said to give the Holy Spirit to his disciples to equip them for their mission (20.22-23). But unlike the other three Gospel writers, John stresses that the Spirit *remains* with Jesus from the moment of his baptism onwards and throughout his ministry (1.32*b*, cf. 7.39); and the Spirit who remains with Jesus during his earthly work also dwells in the church after his glorification (14.16-17). The concept of an indwelling Spirit, creating as well as demanding a mutual indwelling between God and the believers, is thus one which John shares with Paul.

The further and particular contribution which John makes to the Christian apprehension of the Spirit's nature, however, lies in his description of the Spirit in personal terms. In the 'farewell discourse' (John 14-16) the Spirit is spoken of as the Paraclete. There is good reason to argue that this word is used to present the Spirit in personal terms as the *alter ego* of Jesus himself. Thus after the resurrection the nature and activity of the Paraclete are similar to those of Jesus before his glorification. But while in these chapters the Paraclete is *like* Jesus, acting for him in the early Christian community, he is also *distinguished* from Jesus. He is sent by Jesus to the disciples from the Father. Indeed he is explicitly identified as the Holy Spirit (14.26), who after the exaltation of Christ helps his followers. By thus personalising the Spirit, and also seeing him as the distinct *alter ego* of the divine Son of God, John goes much further than other New Testament writers, including Paul, and moves the Christian understanding of the Holy Spirit in a direction which eventually produces the trinitarian formula of God.

The New Testament views of the Spirit, we may conclude, build on Old Testament teaching and develop it. In so doing the Christian perception of the Spirit adds significantly to the understanding of God himself which was developing in the early church. In the light of the incarnation and glorification of Jesus Christ the Spirit of God is thought of not only as the outgoing power and presence of God, but also as personal in a manner which distinguishes him from both Jesus and God. This thinking moves beyond the Old Testament view of the Spirit as the transcendent God intervening from time to time in his creation to an understanding of the Spirit as abiding in the life of the Christian community and of the individual believer, inspiring both, and transforming them into the likeness of Christ.

CONCLUSION

We can now draw together the threads of this chapter, in which we have been thinking of the effects of the coming of Jesus on the disciples' understanding of God. This coming brought a new realisation of God's accessibility, a recognition of his entrance into human suffering and of his relationship to his people, and at the same time a new estimate of the persons of Christ and of the Spirit in relation to God himself.

The Christian story is a story of grace, the grace of God's kingdom preached by Jesus and demonstrated in his sacrificial death. From the very first the disciples proclaimed that he was risen and exalted as the Messiah and Son of God. Thus the cross was seen to be the act of God's love, assuring a final outcome in the salvation of all who believed. In making this proclamation, they set Jesus so high, far above the ranks of angels, at the right hand of God himself, that there was a well-nigh irresistible pressure to 'make him equal with God', as the opponents of the Christian message were not slow to point out (John 5.18, 10.33). Yet this pressure could never lead to the conclusion that Jesus was a second god, because it was the love of God himself that had been demonstrated in him, and which had become accessible through him.

In fact the way to a resolution of the difficulty had been prepared by the personification of the attributes of God within the Jewish religious tradition. The Christian idea of the Holy Spirit in the New Testament, for example, is not fundamentally different from that of the Spirit of Yahweh in the Old Testament, although, as we have seen, it has been greatly enriched as a result of experience. Similarly the Wisdom or Word of Yahweh was available to express God in relation to his creation, especially in salvation history and in the Law considered as God's gift. By seeing Jesus first as the expression of God's Wisdom (Paul) and then as the actual embodiment of his Word (John), the unique role of Jesus in the history of salvation could be given a theological explanation by those who were aware that through him they were incorporated into God's kingdom as his children, and already shared in the gifts of the Spirit which belong to the kingdom. Thus God, the God of Israel, is also known as the Father of his crucified and redeeming Son, and in the distinguishable person of his sanctifying Spirit. But precisely because these are, theologically speaking, also functions or attributes of the one God, the unity of God is not impaired.

The beginnings of Christian doctrine in the New Testament are varied and tentative, and it remained for the Church Fathers to work out the implications of them. But the Christian doctrine of God is not a speculative theory. It is an attempt at understanding a profound religious experience, centred in the life and teaching of Jesus. It is an experience which is superbly captured in the words of Paul's greeting at the close of 2 Corinthians (13.14): 'The grace of the Lord Jesus Christ and the love of God and the fellowship of the Holy Spirit be with you all.'

7
God as Trinity: An Approach through Prayer

I WHY THE NEGLECT OF THE DOCTRINE OF THE TRINITY TODAY?

Christians confronted with the claims of other religions may be aware that their faith can be distinguished from other brands of theism by its particular kind of trinitarian structure. It is neither bald, undifferentiated monotheism, nor is it polytheism. Yet the majority of Christians in the West today, it must be admitted, would be hard pressed even to give an account, let alone a defence, of the developed doctrine of the Trinity as expressed in Christianity's historic creeds and the documents of its Councils. Most professing Christians know how to use the language of Father, Son and Spirit in the varied and unsystematic way that we find in the New Testament. There are 'rules' for this language that are generally acknowledged in the Church. Christians know that there is something wholly inappropriate, for instance, in saying that 'God the Father died on the cross', even if they cannot give a coherent explanation of the reason. The way Luke unfolds the story of God's salvation is the dominant influence here in controlling our use of the language of Father, Son and Spirit: at the historical level there was first the Father God of the Old Testament, then the Son, then, at the Son's 'departure', the Spirit.

What many perhaps do not realise is that efficiency in operating the 'rules' of this New Testament language is still a very far cry from acknowledgement of God as

Trinity. Even Paul's familiar grace in 2 Cor. 13.14 is not trinitarian in this stricter sense: 'the grace of the Lord Jesus Christ and the love of God and the fellowship of the Holy Spirit' clearly indicates that 'God' here means the Father alone, despite the close (but theologically unclarified) juxtaposition of Son and Spirit.

The developed doctrine of the Trinity, then, is another matter. This was enunciated by the end of the fourth century, and is implied by the Nicene creed, the creed used today in most celebrations of the eucharist. Here God is seen as eternally triune, which means that in the Godhead there are united three 'persons' ('hypostases'), who are distinguishable only by number and relation to one another, and inseparable in their activity. It is this latter understanding of the doctrine of the Trinity with which this chapter is concerned; and it is this that seems to have lost its allure for the majority of contemporary Western Christians, so that Karl Rahner has justly marked that 'Christians, for all their orthodox profession of faith in the Trinity, are virtually just "monotheist" in their actual religious existence' (*Theological Investigations* IV. 79). Many, that is, if asked to describe 'God', would give a description of the Father only.

Why is this? Many factors have contributed to this quiet anti-trinitarian tendency in Western Christianity, and cumulatively they are certainly powerful. As far back as the medieval period, scholastic theology made philosophical discussion of God as *one* a prior and preliminary task to discussion of his revelation as three-in-one; and this in itself, it has been argued, implicitly promoted an undifferentiated monotheism at the expense of trinitarianism. But even more significantly, people today are now heirs of the Enlightenment. They are not afraid of a critical approach. Many are less prone to believe a doctrine simply because it is taught or because it is part of our tradition. 'The wise man apportions his belief to the evidence', wrote David Hume. Free enquiry must take place, and if it does not lead to orthodoxy, then this is part of the liberty that must be granted to the human mind. 'Whosoever will be saved . . . (must) . . . worship one God in Trinity' is not the kind of constraint which Christians of this generation are likely to heed.

In modern theology, too, there is a good deal to militate against belief in the doctrine of an eternally triune God. As we have seen, it appears at first sight to have been built up from the inherited belief in the Father God of Israel as the one supreme God, through the growing awareness of Christ as God, and of the Holy Spirit as co-equal with the Father and the Son in his divinity. To explain how all three could be God and yet affirm belief in the one God without 'confounding the persons' or 'dividing the substance' was the task of the leaders of the early Church. But today it is nothing like so clear that the evidence provided by the New Testament and related sources demands this belief in the divinity of Christ and the distinctness and divinity of the Holy Spirit in the way it was understood in the early Church. Historical-critical study of the New Testament has here been the major force for criticism and change; and the portrait of Jesus of Nazareth which emerges from nearly two centuries of enquiry has for many become far more alluring than the seemingly alien formulas of fifth-century Chalcedonian orthodoxy.

Furthermore (in the Western Church in particular) the doctrine of the Holy Spirit has received limited attention. For centuries orthodox trinitarianism led to the inclusion of the Holy Spirit with the Father and the Son in doxologies, prayers, ascriptions and most artistic representations. But in speaking of the Spirit of God at work in the cosmos, were Christians perhaps really just meaning God the Father at work in a particular way? Is there any need to apportion a separate 'hypostasis' to the Holy Spirit? Is this not basically a question of imagery and language? Even in the most charismatic circles today the experience of the Spirit is the experience of God with us. Do we then really need 'another Paraclete?' Or is John making this distinction simply to account for the difference between the historical experience of Jesus among his disciples and the continuing presence of the risen Christ in the church?

There is therefore a good deal in modern Western theology to dispose people towards the undifferentiated monotheism which has been detected in twentieth-century Christians. Some would argue that the experience of dialogue with other faiths makes abandonment of traditional trinitarianism an even more compelling possibility. A further consideration, highly significant for an age intent on authentication by direct experience, was put classically by Schleiermacher (*The Christian Faith* II 738): 'The Trinity is not an immediate utterance concerning the Christian self-consciousness.' That is, or so Schleiermacher claimed, the doctrine of the Trinity is not apparently verifiable through religious experience. But this is an assertion which calls for careful enquiry.

II REDISCOVERY OF THE TRIUNE GOD: AN APPROACH THROUGH PRAYER

Most Christians would probably say that their experience of God is not obviously or immediately perceived as trinitarian in structure. But does a deepening relationship to God in prayer, especially prayer of a relatively non-discursive or wordless kind, allow one to remain satisfied with a simple undifferentiated monotheism? Naturally there are all sorts of tricky philosophical difficulties about this line of approach. The phenomenon of prayer is varied, and certainly not easy to describe with exactitude. Further, its interpretation is inevitably affected by certain cherished concepts (e.g., biblical ideas, tradition and liturgy), so that there is some circularity in the attempt to capture in terms of doctrine what may be happening. Moreover, competing interpretations abound for so-called 'contemplative' experiences (including the Buddhist way of eliminating the concept of God altogether). But this does not mean that it is impossible to find in the activity of Christian prayer some telling experiential basis for trinitarian reflection.

What is it that Christians who attend silently to God discover? We are not talking of some 'contemplative' elite, but of anyone who regularly spends even a very short time in a quiet waiting upon God. Often, it must be admitted, what will be encountered is darkness, obscurity and distraction. It is no wonder that the experience has such a strange lack of obvious content, for the relationship is one unlike any other, one that relates those who pray to that without which they would not be in being at all. It is (and here Schleiermacher was surely right) a relationship of 'absolute dependence'. Yet perhaps, amid the obscurity, a little more may be said. Usually it dawns bit by bit on the person praying that this activity, which at first seems all one's own doing, is actually the activity of another. It is the experience of being 'prayed in', the discovery that 'we do not know how to pray as we ought' (Rom. 8.26), but are graciously caught up in a divine conversation, passing back and forth in and through the one who prays, 'the Spirit himself bearing witness with our spirit' (Rom. 8.16). We come to prayer empty-handed, aware of weakness, inarticulacy and even of a certain hollow 'fear and trembling', yet it is precisely in these conditions (cf 1 Cor. 2.3-4) that divine dialogue flows. Here then is a way of beginning to understand what it might be to talk of the distinctiveness of the Spirit. It is not that the Spirit is being construed as a divine centre of consciousness entirely separate from the Father, as if two quite different people were having a conversation. Nor, again, is the Spirit conceived as the relationship between two entities that one can assume to be fixed (the Father and the person praying), a relationship which is then perhaps somewhat arbitrarily personified. Rather, and more mysteriously, the Spirit is here seen as that current of divine response to divine self-gift in which the one who prays is caught up and thereby transformed (see again Rom. 8.9-27, 1 Cor. 2.9-16).

Now if this is so, then, logically speaking, what the one who prays comes first to apprehend is the Spirit in its distinctive identity, and only from there do they move on to appreciate the true mystery and *richesse* of the Son. This too is of course a Pauline insight (1 Cor. 12.3: 'No one can say Jesus is Lord except by the Holy Spirit'), but needs spelling out further. For the apprehensions to be made in the light of prayer about the second person of the Trinity are varied, and only indirectly lead one back to the human career of Jesus of Nazareth, although they do indeed lead there.

First, and most fundamentally, when Christians pray like this, their experience of participation in a divine dialogue is an experience of a God who actively and always wills to be amongst us, God Emmanuel. This being so the very structure of prayer is already 'incarnational' (in one sense of that admittedly ambiguous word), and thus immediately focuses attention on the second person in the Godhead.

But second, and more specifically, in allowing the divine activity of prayer to happen, the one who prays begins to glimpse what it might be to be 'in Christ' or to 'have the mind of Christ' (1 Cor. 2.16), or to be 'fellow heirs with Christ' (Rom. 8.18). It is to allow oneself to be shaped by the mutual interaction of Father and Spirit; and in praying the prayer of Christ, in letting the Spirit cry 'Abba, Father' (Rom. 8.15, Gal. 4.6) to make the transition from regarding Christ merely as an external model for imitation to entering into his divine life itself. Paul does not idly say, 'It is no longer I who live, but Christ who lives in me' (Gal. 2.20). To discover this posture of prayer is to be remodelled by the activity of God in the redeemed life of 'sonship' (Rom. 8.15). It is to become nothing less than 'other Christs' in the particularity of our lives, not by any active merit of our own, but simply by willing that which already holds us in existence to reshape us in the likeness of his Son.

But thirdly (and here the reference to the historical life of Jesus of Nazareth again becomes vital), the God whom Christians meet in this prayer is also one who appears, sometimes for very long periods, to desert us; or worse still (as in St John of the Cross's 'Night of the Spirit') to press upon us with apparently negative pressure, causing disturbance, deep uneasiness, the highlighting of sin and even the fear of insanity. Such are the death-throes of the domineering ego. But only in the light thrown on the activity of the Trinity by the story of Christ is this endurable. If we are being 'conformed to the image of (the) Son' (Rom. 8.29), it is precisely aridity and disturbance that we should expect. Only through suffering comes glorification (Rom. 8.17). If we take our cue from the agony in the garden, or from the dereliction of the cross, then the authentic cry of 'Abba' (Mark 14.33-6) indicates that the most powerful and active presence of God is mysteriously compatible with the all too human experiences of anxiety and desolation. Only afterwards do we come to see that what we had thought to be divine absence was in actuality the grace of divine hiddenness. Fidelity to prayer in times such as these, though not always perhaps very consciously Christ-centred, is the measure of our Christ-shaped love.

Fourth, and equally significant in its 'incarnational' implications, is the disconcerting discovery in this kind of prayer that the God who acts thus in us wants us whole, conscious and unconscious, soul and body. 'We await the redemption of our mortal bodies' (Rom. 8.11, 23), for the test of the authentic activity of the Spirit is the apprehension that Jesus Christ has 'come in the flesh' (1 John 4.2). Though Christian tradition is notoriously littered with those who have evaded these implications, it is truly an effect of this prayer that we are gradually forced to accept and integrate those dark and repressed strands of the unconscious that we would rather not acknowledge, and along with these, all aspects of our sexuality, both bodily and emotional.

But it is also true, fifthly, that to find ourselves 'in Christ' is gradually to break through the limitations of the individualism and introspection that often characterise prayer in its earliest stages. The Pauline language about being 'in Christ' describes a mode of being or a status rather than an experience. But because it is corporately shared, it calls in question the supposed absoluteness of the self as an individual or self-contained entity. For all prayer has its corporate dimension; and to pray 'in Christ' is to intuit the mysterious interpenetration of individuals one with another, and thus to question our usual assumptions about the boundaries of the self. It is to discover that central aspect of Pauline christology, the notion of the mutual interdependence of the members of the 'body of Christ' (1 Cor. 12); it is to perceive the flow of trinitarian love coursing out to encompass the whole of humanity.

Sixthly and lastly, the whole creation, inanimate as well as animate, is taken up in this trinitarian flow. To make such a claim could be reckless. Yet it has often been the perception of the mystics to see creation anticipatorily in the light of its true glory, even while it is yet in 'bondage to decay' and 'groaning in travail' (Rom. 8.21-22). Although concern with prayer experience may at first sight reflect a peculiarly modern obsession with direct personal authentication (and indeed carry with it dangers of a kind of narcissistic introversion), nonetheless sustained prayer leads rather to the building up of community than to its dissolution, to intensification rather than atrophy of concern for the life of the world.

The attempt has been to indicate an experience of prayer from which pressure towards trinitarian thinking might arise. As such it is simply a starting point, and no more. But it is clear that we do not here begin with two perfect and supposedly fixed points, Father and Son, external to ourselves and wholly transcendent, with the Spirit then perhaps (rather unconvincingly) characterised as that which relates them. (That, of course, is a caricature of the 'Western' doctrine of the Trinity, but it is a prevalent one.) Rather, we start with the recognition of a vital, though mysterious, divine dialogue within us, through which the meaning and implications of being 'in Christ' become gradually more vivid and extensive. Thus the Trinity ceases to appear as something abstract or merely propositional. It is not solely to do with the internal life of God, but has also to do with us. The flow of trinitarian life is seen as extending into every aspect of our being, personal and social, and beyond that to the bounds of creation.

This approach has strong roots in the thought of Paul. Despite this fact, reflection on prayer is often thought not to have constituted a significant resource for trinitarian discussion during the tortured years of controversy which led to a normative statement of the doctrine at the end of the fourth century. But was this really so? To this question we now turn.

III ROOTS IN THE TRADITION

Many accounts of the development of the doctrine of the Trinity pay limited attention to the personal encounter with God through prayer. A good deal of the material available for a study of this development was provoked by challenge and controversy, and it is understandable that historians of the doctrine should focus their attention on the proceedings of Church Councils and the writings of theologians attacking or defending particular positions, as well as emphasising the political considerations that often became entangled in the debates.

Yet the resulting account of how the church came to profess first the faith of Nicaea in 325, when the Son was declared to be 'of one substance' with the Father, and then that of Constantinople in 381, by which time the doctrine of the Trinity was given normative expression, is sometimes tidier than it deserves to be. The New Testament, after all, presents varied traditions of early Christian belief about the person of Christ and of the Holy Spirit. It is all too easy to take, for example, the Luke-Acts sequence of the revelation of the God of Israel through the story of Jesus to the day of Pentecost, and to see the pre-Nicene church first establishing Christ's identity with, yet distinction from, God the Father, and then in the wake of Nicaea doing the same for the Holy Spirit. Considerations as to whether the Spirit is in fact regarded by the New Testament authors as a separate Person tend to be brushed over in the light of the strong emphasis on his full acceptance as such in the late fourth century. The tendencies of the second-century defenders of Christianity to think in terms of only two divine Persons, the Father and the Son, are seen as a fumbling after truth. Whatever happened *en route*, the faith of Nicaea is assumed to be at least embryonic in the earliest traditions of the primitive church.

The study of controversy, however, is not without its purpose. Councils concerned with faith in the Trinity were not periodic bureaucratic reviews of a continuing theoretical problem, but were urgently called to meet passionate demands. What was the source of this passion? Why did it manifest itself only rarely in academic circles but all too frequently at congregational level, in the gossip of the court, or in banter over the shop counter? Were all the Lord's people theologians? Or was their argument about their own experience of God as Trinity, and the variety of the interpretations of this experience?

It is important in the first place not to underestimate the degree to which Christians of the first three centuries at least were committed to the regular practice of prayer and worship. People in the ancient world would never have called themselves Christian simply because they believed themselves to be clean-living citizens who dropped into church on family or civic occasions. Baptism marked a clean break with the past. Preparation for baptism lasted two and sometimes three years, and a strict watch was kept over the candidates by their sponsors. The end of the course demanded daily attendance at church; and throughout they were directed to pray at least twice a day (morning and evening, and in some places also at the third, sixth, and ninth hours of the day), and were urged to attend the assemblies of the church in the mornings (Hippolytus), where they would be assured that angels and saints prayed with them (Origen). In other words Christians of this period tended to spend a good deal longer in prayer and reflection than many of their twentieth-century counterparts, and the idea of 'the spiritual life' as something only seriously practised by a special group of professionals was wholly alien to the outlook of the period.

Second, the public prayer of the church allowed considerable opportunity to the congregation for being receptive, for listening and for being 'prayed in'. Congregations at the liturgy for the first four centuries were for the most part silent. There were some responses, but very few. Responsorial psalms were introduced, hymns were composed, but the tendency to leave all the music to the choir increased as the years went by; and, with the increasing gap between the language of the liturgy and the vernacular, people no longer 'followed the service' in detail but simply allowed themselves to be caught up in the flow of the eucharistic action, which was felt by them to unite heaven and earth and to bring them through Christ by the Holy Spirit to the Father.

If we were to say then that the understanding of God as Trinity grew in the early centuries through the Christian's experience of God in prayer, then the opportunity for this was not inconsiderable, and we must now look at this experience in more detail.

(1)   *The public prayer of the church.* Two examples may be given to illustrate the intrinsic connection between eucharistic prayer and trinitarian reflection, and thus to indicate how liturgical usage was operative in fostering and guarding some sort of trinitarian notion of God.

(a)   The introductory dialogue to the eucharistic prayer in the Western liturgy begins with the words 'The Lord be with you'. Recent scholarship has suggested that this phrase is either a statement or a prayer, meaning probably 'The Spirit of the Lord is with you' or 'May the Spirit of the Lord be with you'. The reply from the congregation is 'And with thy spirit' ('and also with you'), praying that the celebrant may be given the Spirit of God in order that he may properly celebrate the eucharist. For a long period the eucharistic prayer was prayed extempore (Justin, *I Apol.* 65 ff), and presidents of the eucharist were chosen (among other reasons) for their recognised gift of offering prayer of this kind. Hence the importance of invoking the Spirit of

114

God, since 'we know not how to pray as we ought' (Rom. 8.26). In another example, this time from the Byzantine liturgy, before the eucharistic prayer begins there is a dialogue between priest and deacon in the course of which the priest prays, 'May the Holy Spirit come upon you and the Power of the Most High overshadow you' (as at the Annunciation), to which the deacon replies, 'May the same Holy Spirit celebrate with us all the days of our lives'. This echoes the same theology, even though by this time the central prayer of the eucharist is no longer extemporised. The experience attested by St Paul therefore (1 Cor. 2, Rom. 8) is here highlighted in the liturgy. We do not presume to come to the Lord's table by our own efforts. We are brought to the presence of God through Christ by the Holy Spirit.

(b)   It would of course be equally true to say not only that the celebrant of the eucharist is conscious of being prayed in by the Holy Spirit, but that the prayer which he offers is not his but the prayer of Christ – in other words, Christ prays in him. This, however, needs to be understood carefully. We could say that the celebrant of the eucharist in Justin Martyr's time was conscious that the eucharistic gift of the body and blood of Christ was given in virtue of 'the prayer of the Word who is from him' [*sc.* God the Father] (*I Apol.* 66.3) (and not by any mystical incantation of the celebrant as the emperor might have heard about the mysteries of Mithras). In this case the response is to the prayer of Christ who prays through his mystical body, the church. In this connection, Origen also notes that this too is the experience of Christians who prepare themselves by obedience and devotion for prayer, who will then 'participate in the prayer of the Word of God who stands in the midst even of those who know him not, and never fails the prayer of anyone, but prays to the Father along with him whose mediator he is' (*De Oratione* 10.2). Thus Christ himself in this instance does the praying, and Christians who pray (cf. ibid. 22.4) become like Christ through their prayer: like him they are sons, like him they cry 'Abba,

Father', and all this by the indwelling of the Holy Spirit. So that Christians being 'the image of an image', i.e. being like Christ, who is the 'image' of God (*De Orat.* 22.4), pray *as* Christ and pray Christ's prayer. 'Now you became Christs', writes Cyril of Jerusalem, 'by receiving the . . . Holy Spirit; everything has been wrought in you because you are the likenesses (i.e. images) of Christ.'

(2)   *Prayer in general.* If in liturgical prayer it is possible to discern the pattern of a trinitarian experience of God, of being brought to the Father through incorporation into the Son by the power of the Holy Spirit, then we should expect the same to be true of accounts of prayer in general. This is certainly the case in some authors. Origen's treatise on prayer belongs to the latter part of his life and was written at Caesarea. We have already given some indication of his understanding of the dynamic of prayer, and it is significant that the introductory chapter is given to an exploration of the themes of 1 Cor. 1.30–2.11 and Rom. 8.26 ff. It has already become clear that, for Origen, it is the Spirit who initiates prayer, who makes us Christ-like, and so brings us to the Father. Origen is also insistent that 'we may never pray to anything generated – not even to Christ – but only to God and the Father of all, to whom even Our Saviour himself prayed as we have already said, and teaches us to pray.' Christ for Origen is always High Priest, always Intercessor, always Son as we become sons, so we never pray to him but only through him. Origen's teaching on prayer here is clearly linked with his trinitarian theology, in which the Son is not truly co-equal with the Father, and for which he was later censured. It cannot therefore be claimed that those who pray aright end up inexorably in trinitarian orthodoxy. But it can at least be said that any genuine experience of Christian prayer involves an encounter with God perceived as in some sense triune.

Basil the Great's treatise *On the Holy Spirit*, on the other hand, recounts a similar experience with a modified conclusion in the direction of a more traditional

God as Trinity: An Approach through Prayer

orthodoxy. On first reading it is a keenly dogmatic work written in the heat of controversy, with a good deal of invective against the poor logic of the heretics. Well known (and often greatly disliked) for his defence of Nicene orthodoxy, Basil appears here as a staunch defender of tradition, not least of the baptismal formulas of the church, with the result that one could read him as a person with 'party' interests and a merely intellectual grasp of the position he feels bound to defend. From what we know of his life, this is clearly to underestimate him. Given to the monastic life from an early period, and never as archbishop abandoning his ascetic practices of prayer and self-discipline, it is not surprising that something of personal experience emerges in the course of his defence. The following passage reflects his personal discipline as well as his vision of truth:

> The Spirit comes to us when we withdraw ourselves from evil passions, which have crept into the soul through its friendship with the flesh, alienating us from a close relationship with God . . . Then, like the sun, he will show you in himself the image of the invisible [sc. the Son], and with purified eyes you will see in this blessed image the unspeakable beauty of its prototype [sc. the Father] . . . From this comes knowledge of the future, under-standing of mysteries . . . a place in the choir of angels, endless joy in the presence of God, becoming like God, and, the highest of all desires, becoming God (*On The Holy Spirit*, 9.23).

The significant feature here is that through this direct encounter of the individual's spirit (or soul) with the Spirit of God (cf. 1 Cor. 2, the spiritual with the Spiritual) we are enabled first to see Christ and through this perfect Image to behold the Father, and secondly, as a consequence of our inner illumination, to become spiritual ourselves through God's gracious act of deification. The entire experience, in other words, is trinitarian; and Basil here is setting out a distinct logic and progression in the roles of each divine 'person' in assimilating the Christian to God. Hence, although all three 'persons' do indeed act together, it is important to note that Spirit and Son cannot be seen as mere alternatives.

IV CONCLUSIONS

What then, may be concluded from the analysis of these Pauline passages and their spiritual and trinitarian significance for the early Greek fathers? We have seen that the development of the doctrine of the Trinity in the early church, though so often and necessarily described in terms of theological controversy and the activity of Councils, has its roots firmly in Christian experiences of God through liturgy and personal prayer. The technical trinitarian formularies that were eventually agreed in the fourth and fifth centuries grew in part out of that experience. Nevertheless they were primarily intended as defences against theological alternatives that were deemed misleading, and in themselves rarely conveyed much to inspire and reveal the true nature of the Godhead. Nor indeed did their original exponents propose them as descriptions of their trinitarian God. Rather, they provided the best available means of protecting from erroneous interpretation something that was to a large degree intellectually overwhelming. Only two centuries after the Council of Constantinople, Maximus the Confessor could express his profound dissatisfaction with the use of the term *ousia* ('substance') about the Godhead at all. His objection was spiritually motivated: the reality of God must of necessity transcend all attempts to capture it, even in these hallowed conceptual terms.

If then it is the experience of prayer, both personal and corporate, which is our primary access to God as Trinity, several important conclusions accrue for today. First, we become aware that prayer must have priority, and that no amount of sheer intellectual effort on the one hand, or authoritarian bludgeoning on the other, will effect a lively belief in a trinitarian God. One may undergo the regular discipline of reciting the Athanasian creed; but to no avail if 'the one thing needful' is lacking.

Secondly, the experience of being mysteriously caught up by divine dialogue into the likeness of Christ, while indicating the necessity for thinking in some sort of trinitarian terms, will never in itself yield hard-edged conceptual certainty. The actual business of prayer is itself so varied that the fact that there are differences between various conceptual models for the Trinity should not so greatly surprise us, nor should the constant impression, especially when examining the mystics of the church, that their experience continually chafes at the limits of the traditional and authoritative formularies. This is not to say that it is impossible to establish workable and agreed criteria for distinguishing good from bad doctrinal accounts, or even for effecting some rapprochement between Eastern and Western traditions. But it does mean that any desire for crude and absolute certainty is likely to go disappointed.

If this is so, then, thirdly, light may also be thrown on the pressing contemporary issue from which this chapter started: that of Christianity's relation to other world religions. For here we confront a paradox. On the one hand, the approach to the Trinity through prayer does indeed point up differences between Christianity and other forms of faith. Not only does the Christian who prays, if the account given here is sound, come to discover some felt need for a particular sort of threefold differentiation in the Godhead, a feature unique to Christian theism; but there are also the further ramifications of the 'incarnational' characteristics of prayer – the positive attitude to the body and to the material world on the one hand, and, even more significantly, the haunting image of a God exposed in Christ crucified, of divine presence mediated precisely through weakness and dereliction. These, surely, are the central distinguishing features of Christian theism. Yet from the same experience of prayer emerges the other side of the paradox. For the obscurity, the darkness, the sheer defencelessness of wordless prayer usually lead rather to a greater openness to other traditions than to an assured sense of superiority; and the experience of God thus dimly perceived brings about a curious intuitional recognition of the activity of 'contemplation' in others, whether or not the concept of God to which they adhere is congruous with the Christian one. This latter factor we can surely ill afford to ignore, however difficult it is to incorporate it into a convincing intellectual solution to the problem of vying religious truth claims.

Fourthly, an approach to the Trinity through prayer has implications for the currently vexed issue of masculine and feminine language as applied to God. This is neither a digression, nor a purely contemporary fad, as any comprehensive survey of trinitarian thought would quickly make plain. It has again and again been the insight of those given to prayer that description of the triune God which is not fatally inadequate must somehow encompass, as a matter of balance, what we are conditioned to call feminine characteristics – patience, compassion, endurance, forgiveness, warmth, sustenance and so on – no less than the strength, power, activity, initiative, wrath and suchlike that our society has tended to regard as peculiarly masculine. Sometimes in the Christian tradition this insight has led to a somewhat curious compensating for the assumed masculine stereotyping of the Father by the use of feminine language to refer to one of the other Persons – Spirit or Son. (In the early Syriac theology and in the pseudo-Macarian homilies, for instance, the Spirit is feminine and motherly; in Julian of Norwich, as is better known, Christ is described as 'Our Mother'.) At other times, and perhaps more convincingly, there has been a primary insistence on the ultimate unknowability of God, transcending all categories of gender, combined with a secondary realisation that prayer also forces us to recognise, at the level of anthropomorphic description, the need for a balance of so-called masculine and feminine characteristics in the undivided activity of all three 'Persons'. (Gregory of Nyssa at times approaches this position.)

Just as it is a not uncommon experience among those who give themselves seriously to the practice of prayer that sooner or later they have to face their own need of an integrated sexuality, and of an inward personal balance between activity and receptivity, initiative and response, so too prayer may bring us to a deeper, more comprehensive and more satisfying doctrine of the triune God. Through prayer God can be recognised both as the creative power on whom all depend for their existence, and also as the one who in the dereliction of Christ's cross is disclosed as enduring in patient weakness, and coming perilously close to defeat. The Spirit who prays in us and is known in prayer is indeed Lord and Lifegiver, but also one who cries 'Abba, Father' with us in doubt and darkness and in the sharing of Christ's sufferings. Both man and woman are 'in the image of God', and God is the fullness of the Trinity. The 'masculine' and 'feminine' qualities (as we call them) which we all share in varying admixture are both of them for us clues and glimpses of the wholeness of divine life and love.

8
God Known through Encounter and Response

It should be clear by now that believing in God is different from believing in any other truth and that knowing God is not quite like knowing anything else. There are several reasons why this must be so, and one of them is that God is essentially and forever the Initiator and Animator. He can never for a moment be simply the object of our thought or our knowing or our believing. In some way he is always the prompter of our search for him, the director of our speculation about him, the giver of our faith in him. There is no understanding of God which is not by his self-revelation.

CALL AND OBEDIENCE

Yet he brings this about without infringing the freedom of our relationship with him or emasculating the part we play in it; and one method by which he achieves this is that of call and response, a theme which runs through the whole Bible. People, both individually and corporately, experience God as the One who calls at a particular time and with a specific demand. Individually or corporately they are free to respond or to refuse. If they obey, they learn through the exigencies and the rewards of their fidelity more than they knew before about the God who issued the summons and was with them in the enterprise. Thus, the God who reveals himself to Moses as 'I AM' also says, 'Come now, I will send you to Pharaoh', and it is through Moses' eventual (and rather unwilling) response to this edict that he comes to that profounder knowledge of God which makes him the greatest of all the leaders of God's people Israel. We are indeed as free to accept or dissent from statements about God as to obey or resist his commands. But it is in the process of obedience that a learning takes place far deeper and more personal than the mental acceptance of propositions, because it is not just a learning but a loving. In the words of the ancient tag, *Quantum Deus diligitur tantum cognoscitur*: 'God is known in proportion as he is loved.' This nexus of knowing, loving and doing appears especially strongly in the Epistles and Gospel of John. 'He who loves is born of God and knows God. He who does not love does not know God.' 'This is the love of God, that we keep his commandments.' 'If any man's will is to do his will, he shall know the teaching, whether it is from God or whether I am speaking on my own authority' (1 John 4.7-8; 5.3; John 7.17).

This 'willing to do the will' which is the means by which we come to know God speaks of an obedience and commitment that is neither slavish nor coerced, but spontaneous. The divine call does indeed, for those who respond to it, have something irresistible about it, but their response is like that of a poet to the Muse, or of a lover to the beloved, or of a free people to the call to withstand tyranny. In our response to God's call there is a strong element of 'We can do no other'. In the Johannine writings just referred to, the supreme example of this is Jesus himself. His own unique knowledge of God his Father is bound up with obedience to his Father's will. 'My food is to do the will of him who sent me and to accomplish his work.' 'Truly, truly, I say to you, the Son can do nothing of his own accord, but only what he sees the Father doing.' 'You have not known him; I know him. If I said, I do not know him, I should be a liar like you; but I do know him and I keep his word' (John 4.35, 5.19, 8.55).

It is, of course, a religious commonplace that good people are the ones who know God best. Then why is it that those through whom humanity has learnt most about God have consistently come into conflict with the guardians of conventional piety? There are many reasons that could be given, but one of them is a certain inertia of the imagination. Every one of us is capable of seeing things in a fresh way and expressing them with originality, yet most of us for most of the time settle for some familiar generalisation. Consider how people communicate their response to natural beauty or their appreciation of one another. The view was 'lovely', and they were 'nice', the moon is 'silvery' and babies are 'sweet'; and how refreshing it is when someone's response, probably a child's, generates the sparkle of a more unusual word! So it is with our obedience to God. For long stretches of time we reduce this to a taken-for-granted convention of goodness, and how startling it is when some individual or some community feels impelled to go beyond that in obedience to a more spontaneous, more exacting vocation!

Having the will to do God's will means something more specific than 'I will be good'. Even if it is only crossing the road, like the Good Samaritan, to take responsibility for someone else's need, it involves a change of direction, and perseverance in some venture of which the limits are not yet defined. This is how 'willing to do the will' becomes a discovery of God. Simone Weil was a young teacher of philosophy with an exceptional purity of intellect that would allow no sentiment or inclination to distort the honesty of her pursuit of truth. She became convinced that this pursuit

> is not only defined by a code of morals common to all, but that for each one it consists of a succession of acts and events which are strictly personal to him, and so essential that he who leaves them on one side never reaches the goal . . . and not to follow such an impulse when it made itself felt, even if it demanded impossibilities, seemed to me the greatest of all ills. Hence my conception of obedience; and I put this conception to the test when I entered the factory and stayed on there.

Her experience as a factory worker branded her with a profound sense of affliction, her own and that of others. It was in the midst of this affliction, the fruit of her obedience to that specific vocation, that, as she was reciting a poem for her comfort, Christ himself came down and took possession of her. Of that moment of revelation she wrote: 'In my arguments about the insolubility of the problem of God I had never foreseen the possibility of that, of a real contact person to person, here below, between a human being and God.'

The 'willing to do the will' by which we come to the knowledge of God need not involve anything so dramatic or devastating as this. But however small-scale and mundane the divine demands may be, our response will involve us in some kind of break-out from a routine. Sometimes the first steps are so imperceptible that we do not realise how deeply we have committed ourselves until it is too late to turn back without breaking faith. This happens especially when those first steps in obedience have brought us into fellowship with others who are already more consciously committed. Those whose personal experience has led them, for example, to be concerned for sufferers from a particular illness, or for victims of some social problem, will recognise this process of being drawn imperceptibly into a deeper and deeper involvement. It seems to have been like this for many of the first disciples of Jesus Christ.

So response to God's call is the way to the knowledge of God's nature. It is the real embodiment of that faith by which alone we may enter a relationship with God. The Epistle to the Hebrews, and the Acts of the Apostles in its account of Stephen's address to the Council, both emphasise this aspect of the faith of Abraham which St Paul had already taken as the archetype of Christian faith. The crux of Abraham's response is shifted from his trust in God's promise of an heir to his boldness in setting forth into the unknown to find a promised land. In the Epistle of James the crux of Abraham's faith is found in his readiness to sacrifice Isaac, but the point he draws from this is the same, namely that faith is embodied and brought to completion through action. Despite Luther's scornful dismissal of James, the same boldness in obedience is the essentially Lutheran concept of saving faith. A quotation from a

Lutheran of this century provides a perfect commentary on the 'willing to do the will' which brings us to the knowledge of God. In *The Nature of Faith* in 1959 Gerhard Ebeling wrote:

> We know that faith is hindered both by a lack of understanding and by a lack of daring, or, more strictly, by a lack of willing. . . . For as not understanding can be the cause of not willing, so also not willing can be the cause of not understanding. In fact, in the last analysis both come from the same root, and only thus can they be properly grasped.

THE OBEDIENCE OF PRAYER

So let us consider some forms of Christian activity which, beginning in simple obedience, tend to draw one into a more complex involvement and a deeper understanding. The first is the activity of prayer. Most people who pray begin to do so in simple obedience. They are called or taught to pray – whether in their childhood home, or at the time of confirmation or conversion, or through a personal experience of challenge, bewilderment or need. Few people begin to pray in a coolly enquiring or experimental spirit; few turn to prayer as simply an option or resource. Even when it is personal need which first evokes prayer, prayer does not present itself as merely one option among others, to be discarded if and when the need has passed. The fact is rather that need reinforces a calling or obligation to pray which was previously neglected or disregarded.

Prayer begins in obedience – as something owed to God or called for by God. If we follow the road of obedience we find ourselves at a quite early stage 'taking in' certain truths about God – taking them in so naturally that we scarcely notice that we are doing so. We take in that God is approachable; that he is not a volatile and potentially explosive power-source which may destroy those who approach too near. When we pray we do not find ourselves afraid of 'touching the Ark of the Covenant' and being struck dead. We also take in that God understands our prayer. We do not find ourselves anxious lest a lack of expertise on our part may prevent our prayer from reaching God or may somehow mislead him when it reaches him. Again, we take in along the road of obedience that God is One – the God of 'all things in heaven and earth'. The practice of prayer does not give rise to anxiety lest we might unknowingly be addressing a particular prayer to 'the wrong god', or lest the matter over which we pray may fall outside the competence or concern of the God to whom we pray. The practice of prayer leads rather to increasing breadth and comprehensiveness in the range of prayer, to a growing sense that every facet of ourselves may and should be exposed to God in prayer and every aspect of the world's life laid before him.

No doubt many people have been 'told' these truths about God before ever they begin to pray. For them the effect of the practice of prayer is to change merely theoretical truths into strong and telling motives for gratitude, trust and a widening sense of responsibility. Through prayer mere assent to truth becomes involvement in, and subjection to, the existential pressure of truth.

But the truth of God which is taken in through the obedience of prayer is not always taken in easily. There is often struggle and difficulty to be met on the road through obedience to understanding. Difficulty arises for some people as they try to pray comprehensively, bringing before God every facet of themselves and everything they know of the needs and distresses of others. If they learned to pray in childhood they were probably taught to aim for such comprehensiveness by praying in an ordered sequence – under successive headings of confession, thanksgiving, petition, intercession and so on. Probably they were taught also to think out, and to identify rather precisely, particular sins to be confessed on a particular occasion or particular requests to be made on behalf of their family or neighbours. In the years of childhood this kind of systematic prayer often 'works well': and so it does for some people throughout their life. But others find it increasingly difficult as their understanding both of themselves and of the world around them becomes more complex and sophisticated. They find that the separate categories of prayer tend to merge and coalesce: the confession of sin merges into gratitude for the gift of forgiveness, intercession for others into penitence for one's general insensitivity to their needs. They find that, instead of saying to God first 'sorry' and then 'thank you' and then 'please', as they were taught to in childhood, they need to say all three things at the very same time, so that the precise content of their prayer cannot be expressed in words or even identified in thought. Thus they find themselves reduced to an inarticulate silence. Similarly, in the complexity of adult life it is often extremely difficult to know exactly what it is that one should be bringing before God or asking of him. A person whose marriage is breaking apart will simply not know wherein his or her sin precisely consists, and a parent whose wayward son has been brought before the courts will simply not know precisely what should be asked for on the son's behalf. So again the aspiration to pray thoughtfully and comprehensively passes into confusion and ultimately into a kind of pleading silence.

When prayer passes into silence it may seem to fail and to be of no avail. But, wrestling with this apparent failure, some people find in it a deeper understanding. For when they themselves have fallen inwardly silent and, in the ordinary sense of the term, have ceased to pray, they have a strong sense that prayer is continuing in or through them, that when one has ceased to be the agent of prayer one may still be the place of prayer. So they begin to understand for themselves the truth of St Paul's teaching about the prayer of the indwelling Spirit, about that divine dialogue between the Spirit and the Father which belongs, as we were reflecting in the preceding chapter, to the inner life of the Trinity. In the silence which is the apparent failure of one's obedient prayer one may come to understand that it is not only or primarily by our human prayer that the world is 'bound with gold chains about the feet of God'. The strong and unbreakable 'chain' is the mutual communication of the Spirit who indwells the world and the eternal Father: and through the obedience of prayer we may come to recognise this chain as passing through ourselves.

Another difficulty with which some have to wrestle on the road of obedient prayer – and especially, it seems, those who follow the road most faithfully and furthest – is the experience in prayer of distress, darkness, pain. It is not everybody who meets this difficulty. Some find experience of prayer a steadily peaceful and joyful experience. For them the yoke of obedience is easy, and the burden light. But for others the yoke can be painful and the burden crushing. The total exposure of oneself in prayer can be almost a breaking apart of oneself: prayer for a suffering world may leave one appalled by that suffering; the 'approachable' God to whom one began to pray may seem to withdraw himself and leave one disregarded and abandoned. No one, at the beginning, expects prayer to be so costly, and those who find it so have by then gone so far along the road of obedience that they continue on it almost of necessity. Some, in so doing, come to an understanding of God which previously was beyond them. The darkness and pain which they experience is recognised as a sign not of the absence of God but of the nearness of the God who is revealed in Christ: the God to whom they have come near is the God who has disclosed himself in the suffering figure upon the Cross. Those who are led along the road of obedience into pain and darkness may find themselves discovering, so to speak, 'what it is like' to be the God who is revealed in Christ crucified and come to understand a dimension of the being of God which previously was hidden from them.

A third difficulty met in prayer – and met at some time by almost all who pray – is the difficulty caused by 'unanswered' prayer. This also may lead in a quite simple and direct way to a larger or deeper understanding of God. One prays for something with a good conscience, confident that what one asks for is good and right and must be in accordance with God's will; but what one asks for is not given or does not happen. After a number of such disappointments the temptation arises to abandon prayer, but many resist it and, out of sheer obedience, continue to pray. Along the road of obedience which continues beyond disappointment one begins to be aware of certain resonances between what one prays for and what actually comes to pass. These resonances are too inexact to be called direct answers to prayer. Rather they suggest an ordering of things with which one's own prayer is not wholly discordant. To put the matter crudely: one prays for the particular and, although the particular does not come to pass, something does come to pass which shows that particular in a different light and alters one's attitude to it. Many people have prayed that a sick child may live, and yet, when the child has died, have been able to see in the death and in many human details associated with it, a deeper dimension of that loving will for the child which animated their own prayer. Having prayed with a loving purpose of their own, they have become aware of a larger purpose which is not opposed or indifferent to their own but which is wiser and more comprehensive.

Resonances of this kind, discerned along the road of obedience, tend to enlarge and refine one's understanding of God's will and purpose. The simplistic confidence that, because such-and-such seems good to us, it must be the will of God, tends to become awareness of a divine will and purpose which, though beyond our comprehension, is yet to be trusted in all things. So the practice of prayer moves away from any aspiration to influence the will of God into conformity with our own, and towards the aspiration to align our own will more closely with whatever may be the will of God.

'Thy will be done' is not a word of acquiescence said with a gesture of helplessness nor a comment on the unavoidable. It does not mean 'May thy will happen', nor 'May thy will be passively suffered'. It means 'May thy will be accomplished, wrought out'. God's will is to be done on earth in the same manner in which it is done in heaven.

THE OBEDIENCE OF SERVICE

John 5.17 gives an arresting comment of Jesus that there are no sabbaths in divine grace. 'My Father works all the time, and so do I.' Jesus had been attacked for healing on the Sabbath, the holy day commemorating God's rest after completing and laying aside the work of creation. But the glad benediction of Sabbaths was meant for human well-being, and that well-being is not to be overridden or suspended by a ritual duty. Such a duty, for all its value, must not impede the compassion which is always compelling, and which is the secret of the divine activity itself.

To the average person the embodiment of 'real Christianity' is the Good Samaritan. Here is one who devotes himself to the service of human need – without regard to the origin, race, class or character of the wounded man or to anything else except the fact that he is a 'neighbour' (i.e. that he is 'near by') and that he is in need: and here is one whom Jesus used as a direct and pointed example to his followers: 'Go and do likewise'.

The traditional manner of Christian obedience has been direct and personal action on behalf of someone so physically 'near' that he or she can immediately receive the benefit. Through such obedience there may come about a genuine 'meeting' between person and person – a meeting marked, at its best, by pity, understanding and love on the one side, and on the other side by a gratitude which is moved not only by the gift or service itself but also by the tenderness and love which have motivated it. Where there is such a meeting, where love in giving meets graciousness in receiving, both sides seem to be blessed: and one might say that obedience to Christ's command has, for a moment, 'brought in the kingdom of God'. Where need meets love, something happens which cannot easily be described in utilitarian terms; the occasion has a dimension of depth which can only be interpreted in the language of theology.

Therefore it is not surprising that the Church has traditionally emphasised that manner of obedience which consists in the direct and personal service of need: and the manner has not become irrelevant at the present day. Indeed it is often recognised even in the secular world that in the great cities of our day the most widespread of all needs is one which can be met only through direct and personal 'meetings' – the need of the lonely, the frightened and insecure, the individual 'lost in the crowd'. It would be ironic if the traditional manner of Christian obedience should be discarded by the Church at the very time when the value of it is so widely recognised in the secular world.

But in this world there are many people in need who are 'near by' in the sense that we know about their need and could do something to alleviate it but not 'near by' in the sense that their need can be met by direct and personal service. The need of the world's poor and oppressed is not to be met by fund-raising for relief organisations, by VSO, or by writing letters on behalf of the victims of injustice. Of course there are countless situations in which such direct help is all that can be given: and no Christian would depreciate its importance. But there is another manner of Christian obedience which is essential if the situation of the poor and oppressed is to be radically transformed in the long term – the indirect manner of pressing and working for political, economic and social reform.

Those who advocate this manner of obedience would not deny the importance of the traditional manner in certain circumstances. They would not suggest that the Good Samaritan should have left the traveller to die, and set off to campaign for better policing of the roads. But they would suggest that the very good possibilities that are present in direct and personal service may also become a source of self-indulgence and illusion. The 'good feeling' that attends a loving action which is directly received may become the actual motive for doing it – a self-indulgent motive: and preoccupation with a need that can be directly met (perhaps for a good meal) may blind us to the real need which cannot be directly met – the need for justice, a fair wage or equality of opportunity. In the seats of power, personal kindness may actually diminish awareness of the oppressiveness and even cruelty of one's lifestyle and social role.

To this, of course, the 'traditionalist' may reply that the more indirect and political manner of obedience also contains moral ambiguities and dangers. The acquisition of power, which is the immediate goal of political activity, all too often compromises devotion to what must be, for a Christian, its ultimate goal – 'the good of one's neighbour'. It must also be recognised that the political manner of obedience, even when it keeps the ultimate goal in sight, tends to become so indirect and professional in its methods that it may make its followers unperceptive of need which is close to them and might be directly and personally met. (Both the Priest and the Levite who passed by on the other side were professionally concerned for 'the good of society': perhaps it was because they were so preoccupied with it that they passed by.)

One might say that the varieties of human need can be gathered into two broad categories – the need for love which can best be met by direct and personal action and the need for justice which can best be met by indirect and political action. What is essential is the recognition that both the traditional manner of response to human need and the political manner are manners or methods of obedience. Both contain moral dangers and ambiguities; but both at their best can be honest and obedient responses to Christ's command, 'Go and do likewise'.

In Judaism there is a famous saying put into the mouth of God: 'Would that they forgot me and kept my Law!' To be sure, deep and sublime concepts do lie behind Judaic faith. One cannot enjoin divine will and be unrelated to the divine nature. But the emphasis throughout is on doing rather than conceiving, on obeying rather than subtly credalising. 'Hear, O Israel, the Lord our God, the Lord, is One: and thou shalt love . . .' 'Hearken and do . . .' That 'indicative' of the divine unity, terse and sublime, is in no way a proposition about bare number, 'for number cannot reach him'. It has to do with an unrivalledness, where only God reigns over the entire loyalty of an undivided will. It demands not merely a single worship and an anathema on idolatry, but an inclusive fidelity to God's moral purpose.

It is this categorical imperative, the claim of God without an 'if', which underlies the whole prophetic tradition and condemns all rites and forms which substitute acts of devotion for attitudes of righteousness. 'Bring no more vain oblations, cease to do evil . . .' Honour from the lips may hide the dishonouring heart, people using God to evade God, that is, taking his name in vain. A biblically nourished theology is bound over to this mandatory awareness of the divine imperative and, what is equally important ethically, of the imperative as divine.

It is worth recalling how strongly this dimension, in a distinctive idiom, informs Islam. The *Amr*, which 'descends' at creation with the divine mandate 'Let there be . . .', comes down also as the celestial command directing the created universe and mandating the prophets. Indeed, for the whole Quranic faith the divine relationship to man and history is essentially didactic, hortatory, directional. There is nothing more than prophecy. Revelation is guidance: response is in its 'straight path'. The whole of humanity is understood to have been confronted, in cosmic encounter in primeval time, with the question from God, 'Am I not your Lord?' And in the womb of being which enfolded all generations all have replied '*Bala*, yes! we so acknowledge' (Surah 7.172). The task, then, of *dhikr* (one of the titles of the Qur'ān, as well as the term denoting mystic discipline) is the steady recall of this pledgedness to God which human forgetfulness – a Quranic clue to evil – is all too liable to nullify.

'Hold God in awe' might be said to be the central urge of all Semitic theism and it is one in which Christian faith is partner. We are right to see it tempered and controlled by the distinctively Christian sense of the divine indicative. But this distinctively Christian theology of the Incarnation and of grace in no way excludes the meaning of the divine imperative, which certain contemporary theologians, especially in the Third World, have passionately renewed. Rather it is well to see the vital interfusion of will and nature in our understanding of God, and of will and wonder in our presence in him through worship and prayer.

For, as we saw earlier in this chapter, God's command is never compulsive or arbitrary. Were it so, it would not admit of a truly human relationship. The very creature-hood which is duly commanded by the Creator is a responsive personhood only on condition of being moved not by mere order but by consent of will. This, of course, is the perennial problem of grace. Unless we see and will it of ourselves, the 'ought' – albeit from God – is not morally discerned. The divine strategy (if we may so speak) has to do with the sort of imperative which can be willed within our will. No mere power ever established personal relationship. As John Oman finely said, 'God is willing to fail until He can have the only success love would value.' Hence the deep paradox of the command 'Thou shalt love . . .', whether it be love of God or of neighbour. Love is indeed obligatory, but becomes impossible in the presence of sheer omnipotence. If God's relations with us were those of that sort of almightiness, our wrongness before God would be the easiest situation to correct or the most incredible one ever to have arisen. So to take sin seriously – which is the other side of holding God and his commands in awe – is to know how loving is the sovereignty in God which at once makes us for love, and makes us know we are so made, yet also in his patience waits upon our making of ourselves according to this love. The divine imperative is the more awesome in becoming also the human responsibility.

Coming at it from this angle, we can perceive in a fresh way the wonder of the Incarnation. A 'substance' Christo-logy – 'One in being with the Father' – has had a long and perhaps necessary primacy in Christian thought. But a 'will' Christology, complementarily, would say: 'One in doing with the Father . . .', 'in the beginning was the deed . . .', and 'the deed was among us like a tent pitched . . . and we saw the glory'. Jesus saw all that he did as response to God's will, his life and teaching mediating God's will to others. 'What the Father does the Son does . . .' The first Christian believers saw in the love that suffered on the Cross the definitive reading of the divine mind. Within the evil situation they perceived the fulfilling, and defining, of the divine nature. In a setting which epitomised the wrongness of human wills confronted by the divine will present in Jesus, Christians have found the perfect analogy of God. Faith designated that event to be the supreme expression of how God is God. We know God, so to speak, within the 'doing' of Jesus, and that knowledge requires of us a doing of God's will by the same pattern. Thus to know is to do, and to do is to know. Theologically what is indicative of God happened within the imperative in Jesus. Where we learn what manner of persons we are commanded to be is where we know what manner of love the Father has bestowed on us. But the knowledge of that other is only truly possessed in a will to be conformed to the same obedience. As Jesus had it, 'I in them and thou in me'.

OBEDIENCE TO THE HOLY

A third type of encounter and response through which God is known to many is that of going to church; and church in this context means an actual building in a neighbourhood, be it in a city, town or village. Architecturally it may be very ordinary and have little to commend it, but it is itself a bearer of meaning in the community. It is often the focus of all kinds of expectations, not just among those who go to it regularly but also for those who go only occasionally. The building is far more than just a meeting place for a 'religious' minority who use it Sunday by Sunday.

It is seen as a source of well-being in a place, and it has often been noted that if it is in danger of falling down or of falling into disuse money is given by all sorts of people who seem to have little to do with what goes on inside it. This is true not just in picturesque villages and anonymous suburbs but in run-down inner city areas. A church building is seen as hallowing a place and if it is taken away or has its use changed then the feeling is that the place itself has been devalued.

The symbolic value of the building may be regarded by some as little more than superstition or at best 'folk religion', because 'church' should mean much more than just a building. But it remains a phenomenon that needs to be taken into account. There is relatively rarely as much fuss when a secular building which has been in long public use is demolished. It may be the regular worshippers who pay for the upkeep of the building and struggle to keep it in good repair, but nevertheless it is seen by the community as belonging to everyone.

In addition it has often been noted that those who go to church regularly are seen by others who do not go as their representatives. Through them they are kept in touch with 'their church', even if it is in a way that is one removed from commitment. At certain times of the year, Midnight at Christmas, Mothering Sunday, Harvest Festival and perhaps Remembrance Sunday, they will themselves go to church, and on the strength of this will see themselves as belonging, as 'keeping in touch with base'. There is a feeling that everyone has to have a religion even though it may not be clear what function that religion has. In addition, even in new areas there seems in many places to be an expectation that there will be a person who will be 'their vicar'. Upon him, too, various expectations are placed, and he is judged by the way he lives up to them. Often the idea of what a vicar is and does may be very inadequate, but it is always assumed that there is a relatedness which is not dependent even upon knowing the vicar's name.

Inevitably the church building is the place for important and well-remembered events. Family baptisms, weddings and funerals and the jumble of memories that go with them are all held together by the building. To a casual observer they seem to be quite different events, long separated in time, but for the family involved they are episodes which hang together.

We Believe in God

. . . because it held unspilt
So long and equably what since is found
Only in separation – marriage and birth,
And Death, and thoughts of these – round which was built
This special shell?
(Philip Larkin, 'Church Going', *The Less Deceived*, Marvell Press, p. 29)

This inter-relatedness between people and places finds expression in other ways. Some places are remembered because events of significance happened in them to individuals, groups or nations. They are visited by people who are too easily dismissed simply as tourists, who go in fact for some deeper reason than they are themselves aware of; and they find that in some strange way the place engages them in a way they cannot account for or describe.

In the case of the Holy Place, however, there is another dimension. God is found there, and is experienced in a direct and particular way which does not happen elsewhere. It is easy to dismiss this experience as purely subjective; yet there is evidence that, for some people anyway, their lives have been changed by their visit. They say that it was the place itself that spoke to them. It could be the Holy Places in Jerusalem, Lourdes, Iona, Glastonbury or Lindisfarne, or a host of others, but these centres of pilgrimage have a significance which shapes their lives and in memory is cherished and visited time and time again.

This sense of the holy in a place is not an experience shared by everyone, but it does extend to other areas of experience. A hymn sung to a particular tune, a version of the Bible, can carry a sense of the holy which to a person who does not feel in the same way is no more than sentiment or superstition. The strength of feeling which is thus called out is often surprisingly deep. The fact that Christians of different traditions revere different places, books, etc. is secondary, as is the fact that these feelings are not limited to those who expressly believe the Christian faith. What they have in common is the idea that it is right to defend certain things passionately and often sacrificially

138

not for utilitarian reasons but because that is the response that seems to be demanded by the person, thing or place in question. It is holy. God is to be found within it.

The encounter with the holy is not to be found only in places which can have a 'religious' label put upon them. Indeed, as Alister Hardy points out, 'Contrary to the premise on which most Christian evangelism is planned the awareness of God's presence has little to do with preaching or teaching. It is most often found in solitude and is triggered by natural beauty, music or literature, or by illness, depression or despair.' Some people who have this kind of experience carry on in much the same way as they did before the experience, but a significant number of people feel driven to church because in the church they expect to have these experiences validated and given a context within which their life can take on a new meaning and purpose. For them the meaning of the experience is that they have been addressed by God and it is self-authenticating.

The experiences are all different but what they have in common is that they were unexpected and unearned. This unpredictability can be experienced on the one hand as a kind of overflowing, something that crowns or seals a deep experience, or conversely it seems to be felt when people have come to the end of their own resources and find themselves facing an abyss. Then the experience is of someone who comes unexpectedly and fills an emptiness.

These experiences are difficult to systematise but there are enough similarities in them to form a cluster of meaning which is part of the data to be considered.

Pascal talked of *Deus Absconditus* to describe the sense of the universe being called forth by God and then ignored by him, and certainly this is an experience which many Christians would say they shared, not least in a post-Holocaust world. But, as we have indicated, the experience for some is exactly the opposite, that is of God suddenly making himself known even though until that time he had remained unknown and of no account.

I don't know Who – or what – put the question, I don't know when it was put. I don't even remember answering. But at some moment I did answer Yes to Someone – or Something – and from that hour I was certain that existence is meaningful and that, therefore, my life, in self-surrender, had a goal.

(Dag Hammarskjöld, *Markings*, Faber paperback, p. 169)

A Christian interpretation of this phenomenon is to say that such things happen because that is the way that all that is made has been made. Every created thing is capable of bearing the weight of glory. It is possible to turn but a stone and start a wing, or to say with Blake that everything that lives is holy. One of the features of contemporary life is an interest in conservation and related issues, and with this a new awareness of place in the natural order and the crucial role that this has within it. There does seem to be a need for what Charles Williams called 'the way of affirmation of images' to be laid alongside the *via negativa*, which can help to explore creatively the way that so many people find meaning in the created order.

This sense finds specific Christian expression in the Sacraments which have a central part in the life of the Church. Characteristically the way they are defined within different elements of the Christian tradition is wide and varied. On the one hand their importance is made clear by the fact that they are closely circumscribed and safe-guarded, and the way they are celebrated and received is laid down by canon and regulation. On the other hand there are wide divergences in attempts to formulate their precise meaning. This wide divergence is seen clearly in the different ways in which churches, while agreeing on the centrality of the Sacraments, go about the business of administering them. One tradition will say, for example, that the Eucharist is so important and holy that it should be celebrated only rarely and then with a good deal of preparation, while another tradition will say that the Eucharist is so important and holy that it should be celebrated every day.

To some the Sacraments are tied very closely to the life

and redemptive death of Christ. They gain their meaning
and authority from commands like 'Go and make disciples
of all nations, baptising them in the name of the Father and
of the Son and of the Holy Spirit' and 'Do this in
remembrance of me'. They are the distinctive way in
which the Church remembers Jesus and is faithful to him;
the Church continues to do what he did.

By others they are given a more extended significance.
At the end of his novel about a French curé, *The Diary of a
Country Priest*, Georges Bernanos paints a haunting picture
of the death of the priest. The tubercular figure who had
ministered with such love and devotion to his flock is now
dying without the comfort of the Church which he himself
had given to so many. There is no priest on hand to give
him the last rites. The friend who is with him says how
sorry he is that he has to die like this, but the priest
whispers to him, 'Does it matter? Grace is . . . everywhere', and then dies.

For him clearly the grace that came through the
sacraments could not be separated from the grace which
was present and apparent through all creation. The world
was 'charged with the grandeur of God'. Seen in this way
the whole sacramental life of the Church is a sign to the
whole world, pointing it again towards its own life so that
it can find within it the presence of God.

The very earthiness of the raw material of the sacraments, water, bread, wine, human love, being sorry and
receiving forgiveness, knowing the touch of human hands,
all these things are not there to be taken for granted and
made into narrowly ecclesiastical things, but are to be seen
as some of the ways by which God makes himself known
in the world. They remind people that God can be met in
the everyday, in creation as well as in redemption.

They are capable of being understood at a highly
sophisticated level and yet at the same time their meaning
is grasped profoundly by 'simple people' who come week
by week to receive them. The very regularity of their
coming speaks of their understanding. For them the
weekly receiving of the Sacrament of Holy Communion is

the event that shapes the week and that holds all things together. It is commonly said, 'I do not know what I would do without it' or 'My week does not seem complete without it'.

This coming to the Sacrament has two elements, the first being one of offering, of bringing in their world and their concerns, but more important is the element of receptivity, of being given something, the Body and the Blood of Christ. And, of course, people themselves are often sacraments. A meeting with a person who is holy, or a holy community, is often a profound experience. We cannot define what their holiness is, but somehow we are aware of some extra dimension, of an openness and an availability which speaks to us and makes us feel on the one hand inadequate and on the other enriched just by being with them. There is a sense of having met with God.

This sense of meeting with God, of depending upon him and being receptive and open, which is characteristic of the language used to describe both prayer and sacraments, is also used by many to describe their experience of reading the Bible or indeed having it expounded. It is the Word of God and the Word from God addressed specifically to them. They describe how they have been nourished in their lives by particular texts or verses. The Gideon Bibles put in hospital lockers or left in hotel bedrooms are not always dust-gathering ornaments. It was not just St Augustine who found his life changed by reading a particular section of Scripture at a time of great turmoil in his life.

Holy places, sacred words, sacraments – all not only give to us but, in a strange and often at least dimly recognised way, lay claim upon us. It has often been observed how Latin-speaking Christianity gave to the central acts of Christian worship the name *sacramentum*, borrowed from the soldier's oath of allegiance to the Emperor, just as *Christianoi* was a term about loyalty not about a school of thought. Both Baptism and the Eucharist have to do with dedication to Christ, and identification with Christ. The one is a pledge given in grateful recognition of redemption; the other is the steady re-membering and re-enacting of its meaning and claim. 'It is the mystery of yourselves', said Augustine, 'which is laid upon the holy table: it is the mystery of yourselves that you receive.'

> My life must be Christ's broken bread,
> My love His outpoured wine,
> A cup o'erfilled, a table spread,
> Beneath His Name and sign,
> That other souls, refreshed and fed,
> May share His life through mine.

It was not by self-reservation or remote control that the incarnate love redeemed the world, but by presence and participation. There is no authentic relation to God which is not realised through relation to people. 'When you bring your gift to the altar,' said Jesus, 'and there remember . . . first be reconciled.' Why 'and *there* remember' unless the place of divine presence is also the thrust – the nudge, could we say – of human community? In the grace of the Incarnation and in the calling of the Church the divine engages with the human and the engagement is by action. Worship means the recruitment of the will for the active translation of the meaning of that worship in the real world.

Here, as Thomas Merton remarked in his *Conjectures*, 'too simple a notion of the will of God may short-circuit all religious integrity'. Here, therefore, many difficult deci-sions must be made, which we may not always rightly judge, about what integrity requires of us, as persons, citizens and believers. It must always be a dynamic and a risky engagement with human situations if we are really to know 'God working in us to will and to do' what is after his mind. Certainly it will never mean a mere avoidance of offence, or the supine self-exoneration which protests 'I never did any one any harm'. That indicates a severely private and obtuse world. Instead one of the evident duties of the will that knows God in Christ is – put paradoxically – an appreciation of evil. Early this century R.C. Moberly, in *Atonement and Personality*, wrote the theme of 'vicarious penitence' into the thought of his day. He may not have resolved all the issues it raises. But he set squarely within the will to know God a lively sense of the perversity in human nature. It is urgent that some at least among us should be constrained, as it were, to apologise to God, to be able still to identify blasphemy for what it is, to register the tawdry, the sordid, the devious, for what they are, and expressly resist and refute their unhallowing and distorting of the world and of humanity. To do so is to feel about what is and ought not so to be, what ought to be and is not. 'With everyone sold on the good', asks a character in Saul Bellow's *Humboldt's Gift*, 'how does all the evil get done?' 'Could it have come from us?' asks Edwin Muir in his poem 'The Good Town':

> . . . That old life was easy
> And kind, and comfortable: but evil is restless . . .
> How could our town grow wicked . . .
> and we, poor, ordinary neutral stuff,
> Not good, nor bad . . . we have seen
> Good men made evil wrangling with the evil,
> Straight minds grown crooked fighting crooked minds.
> Our peace betrayed us: we betrayed our peace.
> Look at it well. This was 'the good town' once.

Is it not in such a lively sense, not simply of *mea culpa*, my fault, but of *nostra culpa*, our fault, that we learn a true corporate penitence? This means a will to honesty about the world, its liability to blight and deface its most precious blessings in a rape of nature, or a travesty of sex, or a jungle of politics, or a treachery of religion.

Such contrition, such refusal of self-justification, moves into doing. Liberation Theology in recent decades has certainly focused, if it has not resolved, the relation of faith and society. Some western Christian reactions to it have sounded like pleas for non-disturbance and the *status quo*. But Liberation Theology recognises that there are situations of injustice, poverty, oppression, deprivation, where there can be no honest neutrality. For to be neutral is to connive.

The God of the Bible cannot be grasped as a neuter Theme: he stops being God the moment his injunction ceases. And man has many resources at his disposal to cause this command to come to an end. He need only objectify God in some way. At that moment God is no longer God. Man has made him into an idol. God no longer commands man . . . The question is not whether someone is seeking God or not, but whether he is seeking him where God himself said that he is.

(José P. Miranda, *Marx and the Bible* (SCM Press 1977), pp. 40, 57).

'Where', for the liberationists, is with the poor and the oppressed. Justice has a prior claim over worship and ecclesiastical organisation. Contemplation can never displace command. The passionate urgency of Liberation Theology finds all the meaning of divine transcendence in the moral imperative. Taken at its face value, such a position is intellectually unacceptable because self-negating; but the urgency and passion which inspire it must surely be ours. We must take its prophetic call to heart while at the same time being no less urgent to adore, for the sake of that very same passion and urgency, the God of the infinite spaces and the unfailing stars, of poetry and wonder and ever glad surprise. 'Love of neighbour' is inseparable from 'love of God'. If they are to be distinguished, for the sake of the commandments themselves and our own limited perceptions, must there not be nevertheless a knowledge and love within our will which, because they are for him alone, are thereby ever alerted to his human ones 'where he has said that he is, in the midst of life'? If, in Micah's words, we are 'to do justly and to love mercy', we must surely also 'walk humbly with our God'.

The meaning of the great Vision of Judgement in Matt. 25.31–46 has gone deep into Christian poetry and imagery. 'The poor of the world are my body, said he.' Christ incognito is ever at hand, serving and to be served. 'Inasmuch as you did it to one of the least of these my brothers, you did it to me.' Is not all such compassion, in Paul's phrase, a 'discerning of the body', that body of humanity into which by birth came the Son of Man, thereby made like to his brethren? For the purpose of the parable, the knowing was in the doing even if awareness was first wanting. 'Lord, when did we see *you* sick?' Within the answered imperative of compassion was the secret of the divine presence.

If we would know God in the authentic Christian tradition of his knowability in Christ, we must learn a will to be conformed to the image of his Son. The Eucharist as the apex of our praying discloses the self-giving of Christ, incorporates us into his ministering Body, and engages us imperatively with the body of humankind, there to belong and to act 'in the knowledge and love of God'.

9
The God in Whom We Trust

Few people are more widely admired than those who pass through extremes of personal suffering or public calamity without bitterness or hysteria and with a quiet and hopeful confidence; and if such people attribute their confidence to faith in God their 'witness' or 'testimony' is very important. It may well persuade a doubter or unbeliever to enquire more seriously into the nature and content of this faith, a faith which can have such admirable consequences in times of distress.

In reply to an enquiry of this sort it is not enough for Christians to assert, as the content of their faith, simply that 'God exists' and 'God is good'. The enquirer will see here no adequate grounds for hope and confidence, unless it is also made explicit that it is this good God who is actually 'in control' of the world, that it is by his good hands that all things are ordered and that, therefore, despite appearances all things that happen are included within his good purpose and lead to ultimate good.

The enquirer will recognise that such faith in God's control must be a source of hope and confidence in all circumstances, but will also almost certainly question its credibility. Can it really be by the control of God's good hands that the disaster at Aberfan came about, or some devastating flood or drought or, indeed, the Holocaust? At the very least Christians will have to give some further explanation of their faith that, when these things happened, God was 'in control'. What kind of illustration or analogy or 'model' will help us to understand this alleged control? Is it like the tight control of a computer programme over the operation of a machine? Is it more like the occasional intervention by which a teacher keeps a class 'under control'? Is it perhaps like the distant control of a military commander over an army numbered in millions?

Christians can hardly avoid responding in some way, positively or negatively, to such models. They realise that no model drawn from within the world can adequately express the relationship between the world as a whole and the God who is the source and ground of its being, and that no model therefore should be pushed too far or claimed to explain everything. But they will also recognise that one model may be more, or less misleading than another, and, in particular, that an enquirer's difficulties may arise precisely because one particular model is pressed too far. Even if the Christian understanding of God transcends the need or possibility of models or analogies, the enquirer's probings do not. For the enquirer's sake, therefore, if for no other reason, Christians must be open to discuss in terms of possible models that divine control or ordering of the world which is the ground of Christian confidence in times of distress and apparent catastrophe.

IMAGES OF DIVINE CONTROL

Many Christians would hold that the authentic and authoritative model of divine control is given to us in the biblical image of the Sovereignty or Kingship of God. Certainly this image pervades the Bible. But its force may be lost on the modern enquirer simply because the power of kings is so much diminished and their role so greatly changed in the modern world. What we expect of kings is not what the biblical writers expected. In us their image evokes respect but may inspire little awe. Furthermore the biblical expectation, though greater than our own, is not entirely consistent or homogeneous. Two rather different images of kingship, two rather different 'pictures' of what a good king is and does, appear in the Bible.

One such image appears in the Wisdom of Solomon, and is quite close to Plato's image or concept of the 'philosopher-king'. Here kingship is 'the upholding of the people' (6.24). The King will 'set the people in order' (8.14) and 'order the world according to equity and righteousness' (9.3). He knows 'all things that are either secret or manifest' (7.21). The wisdom which teaches him what is right also enables him to achieve it in his kingdom – for that wisdom is 'the worker of all things', 'cannot be obstructed', 'oversees all things' (7.22–3) and, 'reaching from one end to the other, sweetly orders all things' (8.1). The image is of someone by whose wisdom and power everything is so controlled that nothing can be present in the kingdom which is alien to his will, nothing can happen in it save by his 'ordering'.

In Psalm 72 a distinctly different image of kingship appears, which may be called the image of the 'saviour-king'. In the realm of the saviour-king certain things appear which are quite definitely not in accordance with the royal will; and the greatness of the king lies in the readiness and effectiveness with which he redeems or redresses these things. The king will 'defend the poor . . . defend the children of the poor and punish the wrong-doer' (verses 2 and 4). He will 'deliver the poor when he crieth; the needy also and him that hath no helper' (verse 12), and in his sight the blood of the poor will be 'dear' (verse 14). Clearly it is not by the will of the king that poverty and oppression exist in his kingdom. His role as a good king is to respond to them with remedy and redress, to act as King David is prepared to act when Nathan tells him of the poor man deprived of his 'one ewe lamb'. Unlike the philosopher-king, in whose kingdom nothing can occur which is alien to the royal will, the saviour-king is constantly meeting, redressing and redeeming that which is alien to his will.

So the biblical image of kingship has at least two facets, and both these facets appear when human kingship is used as a model of divine sovereignty. Sometimes biblical writers insist that a certain event, disastrous as it appeared to human eyes, was in fact willed by God for his own purposes. So it was that Pharaoh's heart was hardened and that Nineveh repented when Jonah preached. In these cases God is represented, so to speak, as the philosopher-king in whose realm, despite all appearances, everything happens precisely as he wills and ordains it. But in many other cases it is as the saviour-king that God appears – responding to actions and situations which are alien to his will, hearing and punishing when the blood of Abel cries to him from the ground, turning to good the evil which Joseph's brothers do to him, avenging the death of Uriah the Hittite by the death of Bathsheba's child, punishing the sin of his people or remitting punishment in response to Moses' intercession, pleading with his people through the prophets, stirred to action when they are enslaved in Egypt or oppressed by foreign invaders. In such situations it is very clear that God is responding to what he has not willed, that he is the saviour-king, acting to set right what is wrong, to redress, redeem and deliver.

In the kingdom of the philosopher-king all is, so to speak, 'programmed' by and in conformity with the sovereign's will. In the kingdom of the saviour-king many things must be won into conformity with the sovereign's will. Both these images of divine control are present in the Bible, but it is undoubtedly the second which predominates; and this image, in contrast to that of the philosopher-king, suggests a God who is not only attentive to his people but also close to them, involved with them. The philosopher-king is raised above any involvement in such distresses as his people may experience, because those distresses are actually willed by him for his own good purposes. But the saviour-king is so close to his people that he can be roused to anger by the appearance among them of things alien to his will, and be vulnerable to the grief which cries, 'What have I done to you, O my people, and wherein have I wearied you?' God the saviour-king shepherds his people, leads them, pioneers the way for them out of slavery and the shadow of death. He is acquainted with his people's distresses from the inside. He bears their griefs and carries their sorrows; he shares what his people endure. He travels with his people through the wilderness – even 'dwelling in tents' as they do – and, as their leader, is not exempt from the perseverance and faithfulness which that journey must entail. The important biblical concept of the faithfulness of God suggests very powerfully his involvement in the labours and struggles of his people.

It has already been remarked that kingship in the modern world is not what it was: a modern king dignifies rather than controls the nation's life. Therefore it will not be much help to a modern enquirer if we explain our understanding of God's control of the world in terms of the model of the saviour-king. Can this model be translated or updated? One possible and promising translation is into the language of artistic creation, an activity much analysed and discussed today.

The artist in any field gives being to a work of art. It is he or she who makes it what it is. Admittedly, pre-existent materials are used; but of the work of art as such the artist alone is the creator – it is out of the artist's spontaneity that the work of art comes into being. But that spontaneity must be expressed within some kind of form – a canvas of a particular size, a certain verse convention. The artist chooses the form; but the form once chosen exercises a degree of constraint or discipline on his or her spontaneity. Spontaneity does not simply flow, nor is art simply 'doodling' with a pencil or strumming as one pleases upon a stringed instrument. In artistic creativity a certain struggle or adventure is involved – the endeavour to contain and express spontaneity within form. In this endeavour there is no programme or blueprint to follow. The artist is reaching out towards a vision or possibility which is not yet fully formulated even in 'the inward eye', and which appears with increasing clarity only as the work proceeds.

If we now apply this model to God, we may find that it helps us to approach some aspects of the age-old problem of evil. Having freely chosen to create something in a particular 'medium', God may no longer be free to escape the constraints which that medium imposes. The question why God 'allows' an earthquake, a volcanic eruption, a flood or a drought – things which may take a heavy toll of innocent human life – needs to be set in the context of the fact that the creation of any environment suitable for living beings (which in any case depends upon an extraordinarily fine balance in the chemistry of the atmosphere) entails accepting a variable climate with all those instabilities which lead (from a human point of view) to disasters.

There is, however, a further aspect of the artist model which may take us somewhat nearer to the heart of evil and suffering. At this point it may be helpful to think of a sculptor rather than a painter. Once the medium (a block of stone or wood) is chosen, then, as we have said, it imposes its own constraints. In the artist's mind is a clear idea of the intended shape; but certain unforeseen factors may intervene. The material used may have a grain, a knot or an imperfection which resists the creative intention; or a cut may be made which is actually 'wrong', in the sense of not being exactly what was intended. It is here that the greatness of the artist appears in the skill and patience needed to 'win back' that which is 'wrong'. The wrong is not simply left as it is, as it might be by an inferior artist, nor is it simply eliminated or cast aside – for it is an authentic element in the artist's spontaneity. Still less, of course, is the whole work abandoned. The great artist wins back that which is wrong, works with peculiar intensity to find a way by which that imperfection or error may be made to contribute to the total vision rather than detract from it, to enrich it rather than impoverish it. This struggle to win back, and the capacity to do so, is mysterious and difficult to analyse, but anyone who has ever created anything will be well aware of it. It is the exercise of a special and unique kind of 'control' – a control which redeems rather than prevents the wrong, which draws into the overall purpose that which obstructs that purpose. The control of the artist is a 'saving' rather than a 'programming' form of control. 'Creation' is also a continuing 'redemption'.

The nature of artistic creativity is of so much interest at

the present time that, if it were offered as a model of God's control or ordering of the world, it might well prove thought-provoking and suggestive to enquirers. It is not strictly a biblical model, but there are strong and clear resonances between what it suggests and what is suggested by the dominant biblical image of God as saviour-king. The model suggests that, while the world and everything which it contains is God's work, some of the things and events within the world are 'not what God wants' and are in need of winning back or redeeming into the ambit of his good purpose. To some people this will be a feature of the model which enhances its credibility. It will also be more credible to some, because it suggests a God who, so far from presiding in distant serenity over a fallen and anguished world, is constantly involved in the close encounter of redemption.

The artist-model is not, of course, of use only to throw light on the problem of evil. It is also a way of picturing the creation itself. In this respect it is certainly more adequate than the 'clockmaker' model, which has been popular ever since the eighteenth century, and which still affects the thinking of many religious people today. According to this model, the Creator is imagined as setting up an immensely complex piece of machinery and then letting it run according to its own laws and mechanisms. Everything that happens is the result of something that happened previously, and this long interconnected series of happenings can in theory be traced back to the original devising of the Creator. It was a model which was always felt to be seriously inadequate as soon as human beings were brought into the picture, because it presupposed that the Creator had planned to its last detail the great history of life on this earth, and that, having set it in motion, he was now allowing it to run its predetermined course. Such total determinism, even apart from the philosophical difficulties it raises, has never been felt to be compatible with the experience of what it is to be a free human being; and even as a way of understanding the world of nature, the 'clockmaker' model is quite out of touch with contemporary science.

Modern genetic and evolutionary theory cannot possibly be reconciled with such a crudely mechanistic interpetation of the universe.

But the artist–model in turn becomes less appropriate as soon as it becomes necessary to offer an interpretation of the phenomenon of human life. Even if the materials an artist uses bring with them some constraints, it is still the artist who is in control. The materials are inanimate. They can be selected or rejected at will. They have no place in the artefact unless the artist makes use of them. The moment that among the materials the creator uses are found living beings – and still more if those living beings have free will – the artist model is inadequate. This is the meaning of the story of Pygmalion. If the statue comes alive, its relationship with the sculptor is totally changed.

To complete our account of the relationship between the creator and his creation – or between God and human beings – we must therefore explore a further 'model'. The one that lies to hand is one which occurs in many religions and is of great importance in both Judaism and Christianity. This is the model of parent and child. The parents are (in a sense) the 'creator' of their child; but the child is endowed with its own independence, its own free will, and the relationship of the parents to the child may become the arena for a prolonged tussle of wills. Parents consider they know what is best for the child, and seek to direct it in the right paths. The child believes it knows better, and may disregard or disobey the admonitions of its parents. In the early stages the parents may have to use force or material sanctions to impose their will on the child. But as the child grows into adulthood it becomes physically independent of them. They experience the joy and the risk of letting the child be itself, though they may also from time to time use persuasion, accompanied perhaps by threats of disinheritance or other material disadvantages, to influence the child's free and adult decisions.

It is this later phase in the relationship which has provided the most familiar model for the relationship between creator and creature, namely that of a father and

son. In the Judaeo-Christian tradition it is clearly taught
that, in order to persuade his human child to live in the
right way, it is essential that God, like a father, should
make clear to the child what kind of conduct is demanded.
The father 'legislates'; he provides a law or moral standard
by which his offspring shall live.

But suppose the child disobeys the father, what then?
The model of father and child suggests that, having created
beings endowed with free will, God may well decide to
accept the constraint involved, not reducing them to
automata or treating them as infants after they have grown
up. He then does not manifest his power unambiguously
and irresistibly, but influences them by persuasion, not
by force – and indeed shows great resourcefulness in
doing so. He inspires some to expound and elaborate his
law. He sends others as prophets, messengers and
saints to exhort and influence his erring creatures. He
allows men and women to glimpse the rewards which
follow right behaviour and the disastrous consequences
of sin and error. He is patient with their rebelliousness
and lovingly waits for their return. From this point of
view the Old and the New Testaments have much
common ground. They are both examples of the richly
varied appeals made by the creator to his creatures to
direct their lives according to the creator's will and
purpose.

Yet what happens? The children still disobey, the
creatures disregard the will of the creator, sin and error
abound, the law is disregarded. At this point the model of
the father and child can be used in different ways. How
does the father react? He may simply be angry and
redouble his threats. If his children disobey, they know
what is coming to them; if they continue in their
wickedness, they will lose their inheritance. There is
nothing more the father can do. Everything that can be
said has been said, every appeal has been tried, the
consequences of rebellion are as clear now as they have
ever been. Being patient and merciful, the father keeps the
options open a little longer. He may punish, but he

withholds ultimate retribution. But who knows whether he will not eventually lose patience and disown his children altogether?

But the significant feature of the use of this model in Judaism and Christianity lies in the great emphasis which these two religions place on a further application of it: the relationship is one of love. In the Old Testament this is expressed in terms of the father's continued faithfulness and long-suffering. Again and again, the children turn away from the right path and deserve all the penalties which the father has the right to inflict; again and again, he relents and gives his children another chance. Indeed he has let it be known that he never will altogether abandon them to their fate. Their promised inheritance may be indefinitely delayed by their wrong-doing; but such is their father's love towards them that he will never despair of them. He will keep the options open. In the New Testament, the very point of the contrast in Hebrews 12 between God's discipline and that of earthly parents is that, while human parents often act out of mixed motives, God's discipline is prompted purely and exclusively by love.

Christianity uses the same model, but gives it a radical extension.

On the one hand it proclaims that God's children now have new resources and opportunities for conforming to their father's will. It is God's gracious gift, and not our own capacity for self-improvement, which makes it possible for us to fulfil his purposes for us beyond anything we could achieve by our own abilities. On the other hand, it dares to ask: if the children continue to disobey their father, to spurn his gifts and promises, and to prefer their own independence, is the father not hurt? If the model of father and children allows us to talk of the father's love, surely we can press the analogy and say that the father suffers from the disobedience of his children, that the creator, by loving his creation, makes himself vulnerable to being spurned and abused by them?

THE SUFFERING OF GOD

The idea that God loves his creatures as a father loves his children and consequently suffers when his creatures fail to respond to that love is at the heart of the Christian understanding of God. It was 'through Christ' that God reconciled the world to himself – and Christ suffered and died upon the Cross, as a result of the failure of the world to acknowledge and respond to God's love. So, it would appear, God suffered; and if so, our model suggests that he may continue to suffer whenever his creatures reject his purposes for them, somewhat as a human father suffers when his children reject his loving care for them.

Moreover, this way of understanding God's relationship with his creatures enables believers to confront the problem of evil with a new confidence. Again and again, human beings are subjected to suffering, sometimes in consequence of their own sinfulness, sometimes as victims of totally (as it seems) unmerited and inexplicable calamities. Why, they cry, does God allow this to happen? The beginning of an answer may be found, as we have seen, in the notion of constraints inherent in any act of creation: given that God used his freedom to create a world that would be an appropriate environment for free, adventurous and potentially loving human beings, he accepted the constraints imposed upon him by that creative activity, and is therefore not free to obviate all the consequences which cause us to suffer (though, in answer to prayer, he may obviate some). But the father-model is also capable of suggesting a more profound and ultimately far more sustaining answer. Just as a human father suffers if the circumstances in which he has deliberately placed his children for their good turn out to cause them suffering, so we may say that God suffers because of the sufferings of his creatures. We may even say that God is so 'involved' in their suffering that he is actually 'in' the suffering itself. Many Christians would say that it was precisely by coming to grasp and experience this presence of God within human suffering that they have been enabled to bear it and accept it themselves.

But at this point serious misgivings arise. Have we pushed the use of our model too far? Certain things, we believe, must be true of God; otherwise he ceases to be God at all. If we are to attribute suffering to God, must he not cease to be permanent and unchangeable? Does not the believer, struggling against evil and sorrow, require a God who is strong, trustworthy and constant?

There is a technical name in theology for the doctrine which meets this requirement: the impassibility of God. According to this, God by his very nature cannot suffer; and if our father–son model has led us to say something which traditional doctrine explicitly excludes from consideration we must be prepared to abandon it. But in fact this doctrine requires closer examination. If it is to be taken to mean that God does not suffer as we suffer, what becomes of the person of the incarnate Christ? Are we to say that his human nature obviously suffered mental and physical agony, but that the divine nature (i.e. the Word united to the human nature) was somehow anaesthetised by virtue of the simple fact that divinity cannot suffer? But this is to make a nonsense of what the Christian tradition is saying about the person of Christ. Certainly the classical position (as enunciated, for example, at the Council of Chalcedon) is that the two natures in Christ – human and divine – are distinct. But it also states that the two natures are united in one single person and that therefore if Christ suffered then the whole Christ suffered.

It could of course be said (as in the Theopaschite controversy of the sixth century) that this was God temporarily dipping his toes in the waters of human anguish. 'One of the Trinity suffered', but not for long, while the Father and the Spirit remained as aloof as before. But to say this is to distort the doctrine of the Trinity, to fly in the face of the truth that the three Persons are as inseparable in their nature as they are in their creative and redemptive activity. If one suffers, then all suffer, or better, if God is in Christ suffering for our redemption, then this is the sign and guarantee of the Triune God's eternal involvement in human suffering and human destiny. For authentically Christian speech about God is always speech about the Holy Trinity. To think about God's relation to suffering simply in terms of the Father and the Son as separate Beings with different 'histories' (and to leave out the Spirit altogether) is not thinking about the Christian God at all.

Equally false to a Trinitarian vision of God, however, is any treatment of the Persons of the Trinity as if they were replicas of one another, so that whatever we say about the Incarnate Son can be said in the same terms about the Father. The Letter to the Hebrews, for example, says that the Son 'learned obedience through the things that he suffered' (5.8). Any doctrine of genuine Incarnation must say something of this sort. But Christians, at least in the mainstream traditions, do not say that God as God has to go through suffering in order to learn, develop or mature. In God, the wholeness of divine perfection has always been there, and is being brought to bear upon the cosmic drama of pain and evil. It is of the Incarnate Son, sharing in human existence within Space-Time, that we can properly say that he experienced the authentic process of growth into human wholeness, albeit with the appropriate perfection at each stage.

That incarnate experience, with its intense joy as well as its depth of suffering, is our supreme clue to the mystery of God's relation to suffering as God, but it is not a direct picture of that relation. It offers us a creative and decisive insight but it also poses further questions for theological reflection. One of the most important and toughest of these questions is that which lies at the heart of the argument about impassibility and immutability – can God be affected by his creation, and does God change?

The most venerable theological position is that we cannot admit the possibility of change of any kind in God, since he is perfect and, therefore, any change must be for the worse. Consequently we may not say that God suffers, since suffering by definition implies being affected, one way or another, and so changed. On the other hand we meet in the Old Testament an insistence that 'the Living God' is to be recognised by his capacity to react and respond and adapt his actions to changing circumstances, and to find a way round each new frustration. Such a God, by virtue of creating in Space and Time a universe with some degree of inbuilt freedom, exposes himself to being acted upon and, in that sense, being compelled to change.

THE VICTORY OF GOD

Nevertheless, when we come to talk about suffering, we are speaking of change which, in our human experience, is diminishing, damaging, even destructive. Suffering may leave permanent scars or disabilities, even in those who endure it most bravely and lovingly. Many of these human concomitants of suffering may not be very illuminating clues to suffering in God. But one human phenomenon is of crucial importance, and this is what we may call consistency, faithfulness, reliability. Whatever changes some sufferers undergo, they come through with their integrity unimpaired, their loyalty to those they love or to what they believe in still strong and true. In that sense we feel that they, essentially, have not been changed. Within the context of our human incompleteness that degree of mature strength is usually attained only through many knocks and agonies, for we are again talking about the kind of wholeness we discern at the close of the great tragic dramas. But if something corresponding to that hard-won wholeness has been an attribute of God eternally, then we may see how he remains ever the same even though he takes upon himself the suffering of the world. But the Christian faith is not just that, in Christ, the burden of suffering and evil in the world is shared by the Triune God in his love and compassion. In the Resurrection, it has been decisively overcome. Cross and Resurrection are both of them parts of the one integrated self-revelation of God, and the faith of the Christian is focused upon this double but indivisible action of God in Christ. Cross-and-Resurrection proclaims that divine victory comes, but also that it always comes through bitter conflicts; deliverance from evil comes, but always comes by absorbing the evil in patient forgiveness; new life is given, but has always to be given through dying. This is the significance of Christian baptism. We are baptised, according to St Paul, into the death of Jesus and into his burial, in order that we may enter into his resurrection life and become, together, his Body, alive in this world with a life which is already 'hidden with Christ in God', and will there endure eternally.

It is, therefore, precisely because they are Christ's Body in this world, baptised into the pattern of his death and resurrection, that Christians are those who enter into the long-suffering patience of God, sharing his victory over evil by absorbing it in inexhaustible forgiveness, and waiting with him in sure and certain hope of the ultimate triumph of love. The nature of this triumph is revealed unmistakably in the Gospel stories of the first Easter Day. Jesus returns to his friends in a new and transcendent life and power; but the love and forgiveness that marked his earthly existence are unchanged, and the Risen Body still bears the scars and wounds of the Crucified. To pick up our earlier analogy, in the hands of the divine artist what went 'wrong' has become the central and distinctive feature of an even greater work: 'See my hands and my feet, that it is I, myself.'

The Resurrection does not cancel or merely redress the truth that shines from the cross; it confirms it. This is the eternal nature of divine power and victory, insofar as our human minds are capable of grasping it.

This God does not promise that we shall be protected from the accidents and ills of this life, but that those who open themselves to him will be empowered with the human resources of endurance, insight and selflessness that can turn misfortune to good account. The well-known words of Phil. 4.13 in the older versions, 'I can do all things through Christ who strengthens me', are in fact a misleading rendering. The truer sense, which is also more appropriate in the context, is, 'I have strength to cope with anything'.

That in which we put our trust is essentially the constancy and reliability of God; and this is, in fact, all the more solidly established through this understanding of his nature and his purpose. His faithfulness consists in his unbreakable commitment to his People and, as the Scriptures also indicate, to his whole Creation. He will never turn back from the love which binds him to the world and which remains his way with the world to the end of time. It is a way that embraces the 'changes and chances', in all their arbitrary freedom, within the 'eternal changelessness' of a love that bears, believes, hopes, endures all things. By its very nature that love is at once the source of the grace we need in this life, and our hope of glory in the life to come.

Index of Biblical References

Index of Biblical References

General Index

General Index